GORDON RAMSAY'S

*fast*FOOD

RECIPES FROM THE **f** WORD

GORDON RAMSAY'S
fastFOOD

RECIPES FROM THE f WORD

with Mark Sargeant
and Emily Quah

KEY PORTER BOOKS

photographs by Jill Mead

NOTES

Recipes give both standard American measures and metric measures. The two sets of measurements are not exact equivalents, so use one or the other, not a combination.

All spoon measures are level unless otherwise stated: 1 tsp = 5ml spoon; 1 tbsp = 15ml spoon.

All herbs are fresh, and all pepper is freshly ground black pepper unless otherwise suggested.

I recommend using eggs from free-range birds. If you are pregnant or in a vulnerable health group, avoid those recipes that contain raw egg whites or lightly cooked eggs.

My timings are provided as guidelines, with a description of color or texture where appropriate. Oven timings apply to convection ovens. If using a conventional oven, increase the temperature by 25°F (10°C). Use an oven thermometer to check the accuracy of your oven.

CONTENTS

RECIPE LIST

Fish & shellfish

Meat & poultry

Cheese & eggs

Vegetables & grains

Fruit

Chocolate & coffee

INTRODUCTION

When I launched my Sunday lunch campaign, "lack of time" was the excuse most people gave for not cooking. Sadly, ready meals and takeouts have become the staple for many of us. It's tempting and all too easy to blame a hectic lifestyle for eating poorly, but it only takes a bit of effort and organization to make quick, healthy, delicious meals at home. Enjoying good food is a basic pleasure and there's no better way to bring a family closer together than through cooking and sharing a good meal.

My campaign this time around is to redefine the concept of fast food and prove that anyone can prepare speedy meals in less time than it takes to get a pizza delivered. I have some suggestions to get you on the right track.

First, always try to use the best, seasonal ingredients and treat them simply. Good quality food doesn't call for complicated cooking techniques or garnishes. Take homegrown strawberries, for example. At their peak, a squeeze of lemon juice is all it takes to enhance their natural sweetness and flavor. Equally, you don't need an elaborate sauce to accompany a beautiful fresh fish—a zesty vinaigrette will suffice. As far as meat is concerned, fast food means cooking at high temperatures, so you need to know which cuts are best suited to intense heat.

It is also essential to have a well stocked pantry. When it comes to easy weeknight suppers, I recognize that convenience foods such as canned tomatoes, ready-roasted peppers, and canned beans are useful. Even having basic items on hand in the refrigerator and freezer can be a time-saver. At a moment's notice, you can whip up an amazing soup using a bag of frozen peas, crème fraîche, and leftover pancetta.

Once again, I'm giving you menu ideas, with advice on how to plan your time. The simpler, two-course menus are designed for casual weeknight suppers, while the three-course menus are ideal for entertaining. I know what it's like to live life in the fast lane, believe me! However pressed for time you are, please don't neglect what you eat.

Gordon Ramsay.

PANTRY

A well stocked pantry is essential to fast cooking. If you already have most of the ingredients you need on hand, it is easy to pick up a few fresh items—on the way home from work, perhaps. I always have the following basics in my kitchen:

Oils
Pure olive for cooking, extra virgin olive for drizzling, peanut for deep-frying, plus other oils for flavoring such as sesame, walnut, and truffle-infused olive oil

Vinegars
White and red wine vinegar, aged balsamic, cider, sherry, and malt vinegars

Sauces and flavorings
Worcestershire, Tabasco, mustards (whole grain, English, and Dijon), and ketchup

Asian ingredients
Light and dark soy sauce, oyster sauce, sweet chili sauce, tamarind paste, fish sauce, and mirin (rice wine), canned coconut milk

Mediterranean basics
Anchovies in oil, black and green olives, capers, green peppercorns in brine, and canned tomatoes

Pasta, grains, and noodles
Selection of dried pasta (eg spaghetti, penne, and fusilli), rice (jasmine and basmati), couscous, bulgur wheat, and rice noodles

Canned beans
Lima beans, chickpeas, flageolet, and mixed beans

Preserved vegetables in jars
Artichoke hearts, ready-roasted peppers, sun-dried tomatoes in oil, pickles, and gherkins

Baking essentials
Flours (all-purpose and self-rising), sugars (superfine, granulated, confectioners', brown, and raw brown), cocoa powder, and vanilla extract

Sweet extras
Amaretti cookies, runny honey, good quality semisweet chocolate (about 70% cocoa solids), white chocolate, dry unsweetened coconut, and sponge fingers (savoiardi)

Fresh standbys

I use the following ingredients so frequently that I always make sure I have them in the kitchen. Having a regular stock of these foods certainly helps to produce good fast meals. Add them to your weekly shopping list whenever you're about to run out:

Vegetable rack:
- potatoes
- red and white onions
- regular or banana shallots
- garlic
- ginger

Refrigerator:
- butter
- milk
- strained plain yogurt
- crème fraîche
- heavy cream
- Parmesan or romano cheese
- goat cheese
- cream cheese or mascarpone
- free-range eggs
- pancetta (slices or cubetti) or smoked bacon
- lemons and limes
- fresh herbs (see right)

Freezer:
- bread (country loaves, rolls, sliced white or brown bread, pita bread)
- fava beans and peas
- fresh stocks (chicken, fish, and vegetable)
- puff pastry
- good quality ice cream (including vanilla)

Other essentials

Seasonings

To take away seasoning from a chef is like sending a soldier out to war unarmed. Needless to say, a good sea salt (such as Maldon or Fleur de Sel) and black peppercorns are crucial in my kitchens. I also use green and white peppercorns occasionally. Invest in robust salt and pepper mills and freshly grind sea salt and pepper as required.

Spices

I also rely on various spices to jazz up sweet and savory dishes. I recommend that you buy these little and often, as their flavor deteriorates surprisingly quickly. Store them in a cool, dark cupboard. I use the following spices on a regular basis: cardamom pods, celery salt, cinnamon (whole sticks and ground), cloves, coriander seeds, cumin seeds, curry powder, fennel seeds, garam masala, ground ginger, juniper berries, chili powder, mustard seeds, whole nutmeg for grating, paprika, saffron strands, star anise, and vanilla beans.

Herbs

I cannot imagine cooking without fresh herbs to hand. Grow a selection of herbs—a bay tree, rosemary, sage, parsley, mint, chives etc—in the back yard if you can. Otherwise keep little pots of growing herbs on the windowsill— even tender basil, Italian parsley, and cilantro will thrive during the warmer months. In winter, buy parsley, thyme, and cilantro in bunches from a greengrocer or market rather than in packages from a supermarket if you can.

Spirits, liqueurs, and wine

Many a dish is improved with a generous splash of alcohol. In addition to red and white wine, I'd recommend keeping a good bottle of brandy, Cognac, or Calvados; Marsala or Madeira; amaretto liqueur and rum; plus a sweet dessert wine, such as Muscat or Vin Santo.

fast 5 soups

Leek, potato & smoked haddock soup
Pea & mint soup with prosciutto
Lima bean, chorizo & red onion soup
Chilled melon soup with crab garnish
Beet soup with smoked duck

Leek, potato & smoked haddock soup

Serves 4

3 tbsp (45ml) olive oil, plus extra
   to drizzle
2 large leeks, trimmed and thinly sliced
1lb 2oz (500g) Charlotte potatoes, peeled
   and cut into ½-inch (1cm) cubes
1 tsp (5ml) curry powder
sea salt and black pepper
1¾ cups (425ml) milk (whole or lowfat)
1¼ cups (300ml) fish or vegetable stock
1 bay leaf
9oz (250g) smoked haddock fillets
piece of butter
small bunch of chives, minced

Heat the olive oil in a large pan and sauté the leeks, potatoes, curry powder, and seasoning over medium heat for 5 minutes or until the leeks have softened. Add the milk, stock, and bay leaf, bring to a boil, then simmer for 5 minutes until the potatoes are tender.

Add the fish and poach for 2 to 3 minutes until flaky. Lift out with a slotted spoon and break into large flakes, removing the skin. Transfer a quarter of the leeks and potatoes to a bowl, add the butter, and crush lightly with a fork. Stir through the haddock and chives.

Discard the bay leaf and whiz the soup with a blender until smooth and creamy. Check the seasoning and reheat, adding a little extra hot stock or water to thin if needed. Pile the crushed potato and haddock mixture in the center of warm bowls and pour the soup around. Drizzle with a little olive oil and serve.

Pea & mint soup with prosciutto

Serves 4

2 tbsp (30ml) olive oil, plus extra
  to drizzle
4 slices of prosciutto, chopped
sea salt and black pepper
large handful of mint (about 6 sprigs),
  leaves only
1lb 2oz (500g) peas (fresh or frozen)
generous ¾ cup (175ml) crème fraîche

Heat the olive oil in a skillet. Sprinkle the prosciutto with black pepper and cook over high heat until golden brown and crisp, turning once. Drain in a colander, then on paper towels to remove all excess oil.

Add the mint leaves to a medium pan of boiling salted water. Bring back to a boil, then add the peas and blanch for 2 to 3 minutes until they are just tender and still bright green. Drain, reserving the liquor.

Tip the peas and mint into a blender. Add just enough of the hot liquor (about 2 cups/500ml) to cover and whiz to a smooth purée. Add a generous drizzle of olive oil and all but 4 tbsp (60ml) crème fraîche. Season with salt and pepper to taste and pulse for a few seconds to combine.

Pour the soup into warm bowls and dollop the reserved crème fraîche on top. Scatter over the crispy prosciutto and serve.

Lima bean, chorizo & red onion soup

Serves 4

8oz (225g) chorizo sausage, skin removed

3 tbsp (45ml) olive oil, plus extra
  to drizzle

2 red onions, peeled and minced

2 garlic cloves, peeled and very finely
  sliced

few thyme sprigs

2 x 14oz (398g) cans lima beans, drained
  and rinsed

sea salt and black pepper

squeeze of lemon juice

large handful of Italian parsley,
  roughly chopped

Chop the chorizo into small bite-size pieces. Put the kettle on to boil.

Heat the olive oil in a heavy pan and add the onions, garlic, and thyme. Cook, stirring, for 2 minutes, then add the chorizo. Stir over high heat for a few minutes until the oil has taken on a reddish-golden hue from the chorizo.

Tip in the lima beans and pour in just enough boiling water to cover them. Bring to a simmer and cook gently for about 10 minutes.

Season generously with salt and pepper and add a squeeze of lemon juice. Scatter over the chopped parsley and ladle the soup into warm bowls to serve.

Chilled melon soup with crab garnish

Serves 4

2 Charentais (or cantaloupe) melons, chilled
4 tbsp (60ml) plain yogurt

CRAB GARNISH:
5oz (150g) white crabmeat
½ shallot, peeled and minced
½ crisp apple (eg Granny Smith), peeled and finely diced
few cilantro leaves, chopped, plus extra to garnish
1 tbsp (15ml) whole grain mustard
2–3 tbsp (30–45ml) mayonnaise
squeeze of lime juice
sea salt and black pepper

Halve the melons, seed, and peel, then cut into chunks. Tip into a blender and add the yogurt, 6–7 ice cubes and a tiny pinch of salt. Whiz to a very smooth purée. Pour into a bowl and place in the freezer to chill while you prepare the crab.

Put the crabmeat into a bowl and run your fingers through it to pick out any bits of shell. Add the shallot, apple, and chopped cilantro, then stir in the mustard and enough mayonnaise to bind the mixture together. Add lime juice and season with salt and pepper to taste.

To serve, place a large dollop of crabmeat in the center of each chilled soup bowl. Pour the cold melon soup around and garnish with a few cilantro leaves.

Beet soup with smoked duck

Serves 4

3–4 tbsp (45–60ml) olive oil, plus extra
   to drizzle
1 onion, peeled and chopped
1 bay leaf
2 garlic cloves, peeled and crushed
2 large carrots, peeled and chopped
1 celery stalk, trimmed and chopped
1lb (450g) ready-cooked beets
2½ cups (625ml) hot vegetable or chicken
   stock
sea salt and black pepper
squeeze of lemon juice
7oz (200g) smoked duck breasts, thinly
   sliced
sour cream, to drizzle

Heat a large pan and pour in the olive oil. Add the
onion, bay leaf, garlic, carrots, and celery. Cook over high heat, stirring
often, for 4 to 5 minutes until the vegetables begin to soften.

Meanwhile, coarsely grate the beets (wearing rubber
gloves to prevent your hands from staining). Add to the pan and pour
in the stock. Cover and simmer for 10 minutes until the vegetables are
tender. Discard the bay leaf.

Whiz the soup to a smooth purée using a hand-held
(or freestanding) blender. Taste and adjust the seasoning with salt,
pepper, and lemon juice. Reheat gently if necessary.

Ladle the soup into warm bowls. Lay the smoked duck
slices on top and drizzle over the sour cream and olive oil to serve.

Light & healthy

{everyday menu}

I think of this menu as the ideal ladies' lunch—light, flavorful, and full of healthy superfoods. If you want a more substantial meal, serve the fish with some crushed new potatoes. Otherwise, keep it light and finish with a creamy, but guilt-free, blueberry dessert. Serves 4.

Pan-fried hake with tomato relish
Blueberries with honey, almonds & yogurt

- Combine the yogurt, honey, and blueberries. Divide among serving bowls and chill.
- Toast the almonds and cool.
- Prepare the ingredients for the tomato relish.
- Pan-fry the fish and make the relish.
- Serve the main course.
- Top the dessert with toasted almonds and serve.

PAN-FRIED HAKE WITH TOMATO RELISH

> Hake is an underrated fish, which is a shame because it has a subtle and delicious flavor, similar to cod. Best of all, it is environmentally sustainable, yet inexpensive. It is also easy to prepare as it has relatively few bones.

Serves 4

4 silver hake or Boston ling fillets, about
   6oz (175g) each
sea salt and black pepper
3 tbsp (45ml) olive oil, plus extra to drizzle
9oz (250g) vine-ripened cherry or small
   plum tomatoes, quartered
bunch of scallions (about 8),
   trimmed and chopped
1 tsp (5ml) superfine sugar
splash of white wine vinegar
few thyme sprigs (leaves only)
small handful of cilantro leaves, chopped

TIP Heating the fish fillets slowly in a cold skillet prevents them from curling up during pan-frying. This works really well for firm fish with thin skins, such as hake.

Check the hake fillets for any pin bones, removing any you find with a pair of tweezers. Season the fish with salt and pepper. Put 2 tbsp (30ml) olive oil in a cold skillet and lay the fish fillets on top, skin side down.

Slowly warm the skillet over low heat, then increase the heat to medium after a minute or two. Pan-fry until the skin is golden and crisp, and the fillets are cooked two-thirds of the way through.

Turn the fish over and cook the flesh side for 50 to 60 seconds only. Transfer to a plate lined with paper towels to drain; keep warm.

Add 1 tbsp (15ml) olive oil to the pan and sauté the tomatoes and scallions for a minute. Add the sugar and a splash of wine vinegar. Cook over high heat for a minute or two until the vinegar has cooked off and the tomatoes are a little soft but still retaining their shape.

Season the tomatoes well, toss in the herbs, and divide among four warm plates. Place the hake fillets, skin side up, on top and serve immediately.

BLUEBERRIES WITH HONEY, ALMONDS & YOGURT

"We always have berries and yogurt in the refrigerator so I think of this as a speedy pantry dessert, which is also great for breakfast. Toast the almonds rather than buy them ready-toasted—it only takes a minute and the flavor is much better."

Serves 4

4 tbsp (60ml) slivered almonds
⅔ cup (150ml) strained plain yogurt
2 tbsp (30ml) runny honey
9oz (250g) blueberries

Toss the slivered almonds in a small, dry skillet over medium-high heat until fragrant and golden brown. (Don't leave them unattended as they catch and burn easily.) Tip into a bowl and let cool.

Mix the yogurt and honey together in a bowl and fold in the blueberries. Divide among small bowls and chill until ready to serve.

Scatter the toasted almonds over the dessert and drizzle with a little more honey if you like, to serve.

"Great fast food depends on using top quality ingredients. Finding a good butcher, fish supplier, and farmers' market or greengrocer is the key."

fast appetizers

5

Sicilian caponata
Caramelized shallot & mushroom toasts
Sautéed scallops with corn salsa
Salmon ceviche
Soused herrings with curry cream

Sicilian caponata

Serves 4

5 tbsp (75ml) olive oil
1 eggplant, trimmed and cut into chunks
1 onion, peeled and chopped
2 celery stalks, trimmed and chopped
1 red bell pepper, seeded and chopped
sea salt and black pepper
5 large tomatoes
2 garlic cloves, peeled and chopped
2 tbsp superfine sugar
1–1½ tbsp (15–22ml) red wine or balsamic
   vinegar
½ cup (125ml) green olives, pitted and
   sliced
½ cup (125ml) capers, rinsed and drained
handful of basil leaves, torn
⅓ cup (75ml) toasted pine nuts

Heat the olive oil in a wide, heavy pan and sauté the eggplant, onion, celery, and red bell pepper with some seasoning over high heat for about 5 minutes.

Drop the tomatoes into a pot of boiling water for a minute, refresh under cold water, and peel. Halve, seed, and cut into chunks. Add to the pan with the garlic, sugar, vinegar, green olives, and capers.

Cook over high heat for 5 to 8 minutes, stirring occasionally, until the eggplant is tender. Check the seasoning and let cool slightly (or to room temperature).

Scatter the torn basil and toasted pine nuts over the caponata and serve with toasted country bread.

Caramelized shallot & mushroom toasts

Serves 4

6 banana shallots (or 12 regular ones),
   peeled and thinly sliced
2 tbsp (30ml) olive oil, plus extra
   to drizzle
few thyme sprigs, leaves only
1 garlic clove (unpeeled), smashed
sea salt and black pepper
1 tsp (5ml) superfine sugar
14oz (400g) portabellini (or sliced
   portabello) mushrooms
few pieces of butter
splash of sherry vinegar
handful of Italian parsley, chopped
4 thick slices of rustic white bread

Sauté the shallots in a pan over medium heat with the olive oil, thyme, garlic, and seasoning for 3 to 4 minutes until starting to soften. Add the sugar and increase the heat to high. Stir and cook for a few more minutes until the shallots are lightly caramelized.

Add the mushrooms and butter. Cook for a couple of minutes until lightly browned, then splash in the sherry vinegar and add a little more seasoning. Cook for a minute or two until the liquid has evaporated. Discard the garlic clove. Toss in the chopped parsley.

Toast the bread and place a slice on each warm plate. Spoon the shallots and mushrooms on top and drizzle with a little more olive oil to serve, if you like.

Sautéed scallops with corn salsa

Serves 4

12 scallops, shelled and cleaned
½ tsp (2ml) medium curry powder
2 tbsp (30ml) olive oil
small handful of arugula leaves

CORN SALSA:
14oz (398g) can corn, drained
7oz (200g) cherry tomatoes, quartered
1 red chile, seeded and minced
1 red onion, peeled and minced
2 scallions, trimmed and finely sliced
3 tbsp (45ml) sesame oil
handful of cilantro, roughly chopped
juice of 2 limes
dash of light soy sauce
sea salt and black pepper

For the salsa, combine all the ingredients in a pan and stir over medium heat for 2 minutes to warm through.

Halve the scallops horizontally into two disks. Mix the curry powder with 1 tsp (5ml) sea salt and sprinkle over the scallops. Heat a large skillet over high heat and add the olive oil. Pan-fry the scallops for 1 minute each side until golden brown at the edges, turning them in the same order you put them in the skillet to ensure they cook evenly; don't overcook.

Spoon the salsa onto warm plates and arrange the scallops on top. Scatter over a few arugula leaves and serve.

Salmon ceviche

Serves 4

10oz (300g) very fresh salmon fillet,
  skinned
1 red chile, seeded and thinly sliced
1 scallion, trimmed and thinly sliced
  on the diagonal
1 fat garlic clove, peeled and thinly sliced
small handful of cilantro leaves,
  shredded
small handful of mixed cress (optional)

DRESSING:
juice of 1 lemon
2 tbsp (30ml) light soy sauce
2 tbsp (30ml) sesame oil
drizzle of olive oil
sea salt and black pepper
pinch of superfine sugar

For the dressing, whisk the lemon juice, soy, sesame and olive oils together in a bowl. Season with salt and pepper, and add a little sugar to taste.

Slice the salmon and arrange on serving plates, overlapping the slices very slightly. Scatter over the red chile, scallion, and garlic. Spoon over the dressing and let marinate for 5 to 10 minutes.

Scatter the cilantro over the ceviche when you are ready to serve and garnish with mixed cress, if you like.

Soused herrings with curry cream

Serves 4

4 x 9½oz (270g) jars rollmops with onions

⅔ cup (150ml) crème fraîche

1–2 tbsp (15–30ml) no-cook masala curry paste

sea salt and black pepper

4 handfuls of mixed salad leaves (arugula, oak leaf, frisée etc)

1 lemon, quartered

Drain the rollmops and open out the herrings, separating the fillets from the onions. Arrange two rows of onion on each serving plate and lay the herring fillets, skin side up, on top.

Mix the crème fraîche and 1 tbsp (15ml) curry paste together and season with salt and pepper. Taste and add a little more curry paste if you prefer more of a kick.

Drizzle the curry cream over the herring fillets. Arrange a pile of salad leaves on each plate and serve, with lemon wedges on the side.

A taste of Morocco
{entertaining menu}

Slow-cooked aromatic tagines typify this cuisine, but here I've created a Moroccan-inspired quick menu. Serve warm flatbread with the grilled eggplants, and accompany the porgy with couscous. A fragrant orange dessert is the ideal refreshing finish. Serves 4.

Grilled eggplant with sesame seed dressing
Porgy with chermoula
+ couscous   + mixed salad
Fragrant orange slices

- Prepare oranges, dress with honey and orange blossom water, then chill.
- Grill the eggplant.
- Make the sesame seed dressing.
- Prepare the fish and chermoula.
- Put the fish in the oven to bake.
- Prepare the couscous and salad.
- Dress the eggplant with the sesame seed dressing and serve.
- Serve the fish with the chermoula and accompaniments.
- Scatter the cinnamon and nuts over the oranges and serve.

GRILLED EGGPLANT
WITH SESAME SEED DRESSING

" I love this simple Moroccan dish. It makes a delicious appetizer and you can even prepare it a day ahead—just remember to take it out of the refrigerator 20 minutes before serving as it is best eaten at room temperature. "

Serves 4

1 large eggplant, trimmed
olive oil, to brush and drizzle
sea salt and black pepper
few rosemary sprigs, plus extra to garnish
3 bay leaves, plus extra to garnish
juice of ½ lemon

SESAME SEED DRESSING:

1 tbsp (15ml) tahini (sesame seed paste)
2 tbsp (30ml) plain yogurt
1 tbsp (15ml) lemon juice
1 tsp (5ml) runny honey
1 garlic clove, peeled and finely crushed

TIP This sesame seed dressing is equally good with grilled lamb and chicken. Make up a double quantity and store in a jar in the refrigerator; it will keep for a few days.

Cut the eggplant into ½-inch (1cm) thick slices. Generously brush with olive oil on both sides and rub all over with salt and pepper. Toss with the rosemary and bay leaves.

Heat a griddle or a stovetop grill pan, then add the eggplant slices with the herbs. Grill for 4 to 5 minutes on each side until cooked. Transfer to a serving bowl and, while still warm, drizzle over some more olive oil and the lemon juice. Toss well to coat and set aside to cool.

For the dressing, mix all the ingredients together in a bowl until smooth. Stir in 1–2 tbsp (15–30ml) hot water to loosen the dressing until it is the consistency of thick whipping cream. Season to taste with salt and pepper.

Drizzle the dressing over the grilled eggplant and garnish with a few fresh bay leaves and rosemary sprigs. Serve some warm flatbread on the side.

PORGY WITH CHERMOULA

" I think of Moroccan chermoula as the spicy equivalent of an Italian gremolata. Both include garlic, lemon juice, and olive oil, but chermoula is spiked with the heady fragrance of cumin, coriander, and paprika. It can be used as a marinade or simply as a zesty sauce to spoon over fish dishes, such as mouthwatering baked porgy. "

Serves 4

2 porgies, about 1½lb (700g) each,
   scaled and cleaned
sea salt and black pepper
handful of rosemary sprigs
handful of thyme sprigs
2 lemons, sliced
olive oil, to drizzle

CHERMOULA:
2 tsp (10ml) cumin seeds
2 tsp (10ml) coriander seeds
2 garlic cloves, peeled and grated
   or roughly chopped
1 tsp (5ml) sweet paprika
finely grated zest and juice of ½ lemon
4 tbsp (60ml) extra virgin olive oil
large handful of cilantro leaves,
   roughly chopped

Heat the oven to 425°F (220°C). Score the fish on both sides at ¾-inch (2cm) intervals and rub with a little salt and pepper. Stuff the cavity of each fish with a sprig each of rosemary and thyme.

Scatter the lemon slices and a few herb sprigs over the base of one large (or two smaller) sturdy roasting pan(s) and drizzle with olive oil. Place the fish on top and scatter over the remaining herbs. Drizzle a little more olive oil over the fish and season again with salt and pepper.

To prepare the chermoula, toast the cumin and coriander seeds in a skillet over low heat until they release their fragrance. Tip into a mortar and grind to a powder with the pestle. Add the garlic, paprika, a pinch of salt, and a grinding of pepper. Pound to a paste, then stir in the rest of the ingredients, adding the cilantro at the end.

Bake the fish in the oven for about 15 to 20 minutes until it is just cooked through. It's ready when the thickest part of the flesh comes away easily from the bone.

Transfer the porgy to a large warm serving platter. Dress the fish with the chermoula as you fillet them to serve.

FRAGRANT ORANGE SLICES

" This simple, refreshing orange salad is often served as a dessert in Morocco, where it is usual to end a meal with fresh fruit and nuts. The orange blossom water enhances the flavor and fragrance. **"**

Serves 4

4 large oranges
1½ tbsp (22ml) runny honey
1 tbsp (15ml) orange blossom water
pinch of ground cinnamon
½ cup (125ml) toasted walnuts (or pistachios), roughly chopped

Slice off the top and bottom of each orange
and place upright on a cutting board. Following the curve of the fruit, cut off the skin, making sure that you remove the white pith as well. Turn the peeled orange on one side and cut into slices, removing any pips as you do so.

Arrange the orange slices
overlapping on individual plates. Mix the honey with the orange blossom water until evenly blended, then drizzle over the orange slices. Mix the cinnamon and chopped walnuts together and scatter over the oranges to serve.

fast 5 antipasti

Balsamic figs with crumbled Roquefort
Bruschetta with tomato & prosciutto
Bresaola with arugula & Parmesan
Marinated mozzarella
Artichokes in herb & lemon dressing

Balsamic figs with crumbled Roquefort

Serves 4

Take 4oz (125g) Roquefort (or any leftover blue cheese you may have in the refrigerator) and wrap well in all-purpose plastic wrap. Freeze for at least 10 to 15 minutes until firm.

Cut 8 ripe figs into quarters and randomly scatter over four serving plates. Unwrap the blue cheese and grate a generous layer over the figs. Drizzle with some good quality balsamic vinegar and extra virgin olive oil. Grind over a little black pepper and serve straightaway.

Bruschetta with tomato & prosciutto

Serves 4

Cut 6–8 ripe cherry tomatoes into quarters and put into a bowl. Add a few shredded basil leaves, 1½ tbsp (22ml) red wine vinegar, 4 tbsp (60ml) olive oil, and some salt and pepper. Give the mixture a stir and set aside.

Toast 4 thick slices of ciabatta, then rub one side with a halved fat garlic clove. Place on serving plates and spoon over the tomato mixture. Drape each bruschetta with 2 slices of prosciutto and serve.

Bresaola with arugula & Parmesan

Serves 4

Arrange 6 slices of bresaola (salt-cured beef) on each serving plate, allowing the sides to overlap a little.

Scatter over a small handful of arugula leaves, then drizzle with some extra virgin olive oil. Sprinkle with freshly grated Parmesan, a little lemon juice, and freshly cracked black pepper to serve.

Marinated mozzarella

Thickly slice four 5oz (150g) fresh buffalo mozzarella balls. Generously drizzle a serving dish or platter with some extra virgin olive oil, then sprinkle with sea salt, black pepper, and a handful of torn basil leaves.

Arrange the mozzarella slices in a single layer in the dish. Add another generous drizzle of extra virgin olive oil and scatter over more torn basil leaves, salt, and pepper. Squeeze over a little lemon juice.

Cover with plastic wrap and let marinate for 10 to 15 minutes in the refrigerator (or longer if you have time). Serve slightly chilled.

Artichokes in herb & lemon dressing
Serves 4

Drain a 14oz (398g) can or jar of good quality artichoke hearts (or ready-prepared artichokes from a deli). Toss with 1 minced garlic clove and a squeeze of lemon juice. Drizzle with extra virgin olive oil and season with salt and pepper to taste. Let infuse for at least 10 minutes.

Chop a small handful of chives and Italian parsley and stir through the marinated artichokes just before serving.

"A good set of knives enables you to work quickly and efficiently. Keep them sharp—blunt knives are inclined to slip off food into waiting fingers."

Country cooking

Full of rustic, fall flavors, this is comfort food at its best. Meaty pork chops go well with robust sauces—in this instance, a chunky, tangy, lightly spiced tomato and mushroom sauce. Round off the meal with pan-roasted apples and pears—ideally from your back yard or local farmers' market. Serves 4.

planning your menu

Baked pork chops with a piquant sauce
Spiced pan-roasted apples & pears

- **Preheat the oven. Prepare the pork chops ready for baking.**
- **Chop the vegetables for the sauce.**
- **Put the chops in the oven.**
- **Make the mushroom and tomato sauce and let simmer.**
- **Prepare the apples and pears, make the spiced caramel, and add the fruit.**
- **Remove the pork from the oven and let rest.**
- **Add the Calvados and apple juice to the caramelized fruit and reduce.**
- **Serve the pork with the sauce.**
- **Serve the caramelized apples and pears.**

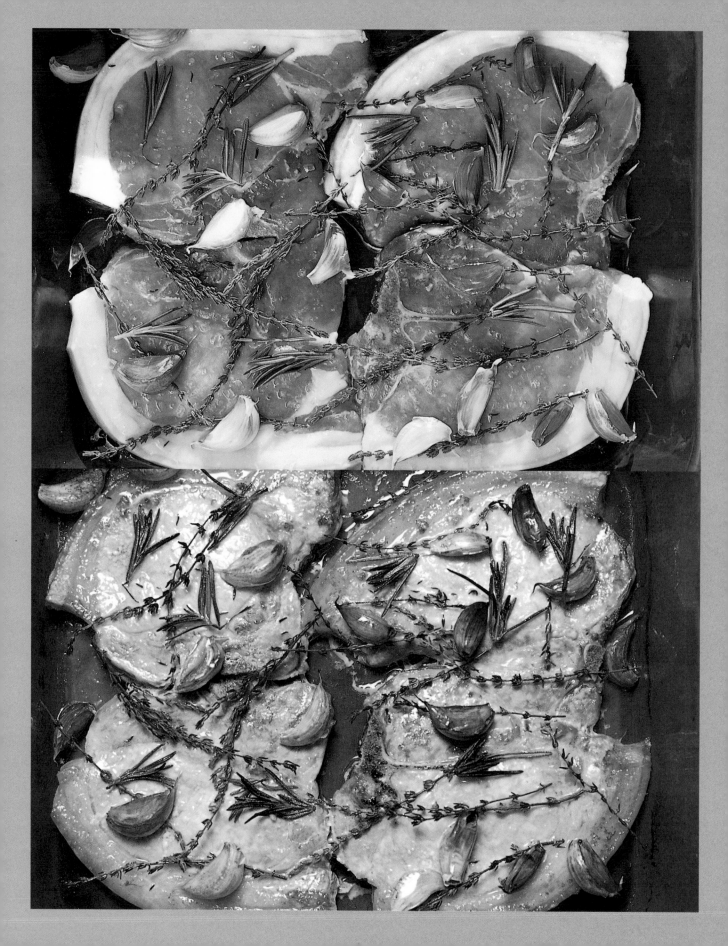

BAKED PORK CHOPS WITH A PIQUANT SAUCE

" These chops are quite satisfying as they are, perhaps with some bread to mop up the sauce, but you could serve them with rice—nutty Camargue red rice would be perfect. The piquant sauce is my adaptation of a rustic Spanish tomato sauce. "

Serves 4

4 pork chops, about 9oz (250g) each
a little olive oil, plus extra to drizzle
few thyme sprigs
few rosemary sprigs (leaves only)
½ head of garlic, separated into cloves
   (unpeeled)
sea salt and black pepper

SAUCE:

3 tbsp (45ml) olive oil
1 large onion, peeled and minced
1 red bell pepper, seeded and minced
1 red chile, seeded and minced
7oz (200g) cremini mushrooms, trimmed
   and finely sliced
14oz (398g) can chopped tomatoes
sea salt and black pepper
1 tsp (5ml) superfine sugar

Heat the oven to 400°F (200°C). Place the pork chops in a large, lightly oiled baking dish and scatter over the thyme sprigs, rosemary leaves, garlic cloves, and salt. Drizzle with a little olive oil and bake for 20 minutes or until the pork chops are cooked through.

Make the sauce in the meantime. Heat the olive oil in a wide pan and add the onion, red bell pepper, chile, and mushrooms. Stir over high heat for 3 to 4 minutes until the vegetables begin to soften. Tip in the tomatoes. Season with salt and pepper and add the sugar and a splash of water. Simmer for 10 to 12 minutes until the onions are tender and the tomato sauce has thickened. Taste and adjust the seasoning.

Take the chops out of the oven and let rest in a warm place for 5 minutes. Then pour any pan juices into the sauce and reheat. Ladle a generous amount of sauce over the chops to serve.

SPICED PAN-ROASTED APPLES & PEARS

"Whole spices lend a unique fragrance and flavor to caramelized apples and pears. If preparing in advance, peel and cut the fruit, then spread out on a clean dish towel to dry out slightly. Don't worry if the pieces discolor a little, as they will be coated in a lovely, dark caramel anyway."

Serves 4
2 firm apples (eg Braeburn)
4 firm pears (eg Conference)
⅓ cup (75ml) superfine sugar
2 cinnamon sticks
1 tsp (5ml) cloves
3 star anise
1 tsp (5ml) black peppercorns, lightly crushed
2 tbsp (30ml) slightly salted butter
splash of Calvados
⅓ cup (75ml) apple juice
crème fraîche, to serve (optional)

Core the apples and pears using an apple corer, then peel off the skins. Cut the apples into quarters and halve the pears.

Scatter the sugar over the bottom of a wide, heavy nonstick skillet and place over high heat until it melts and begins to caramelize at the edges. Add the spices, followed by the butter. Tip the skillet from side to side to mix the caramel and butter together. Take care as the mixture may spit and sputter.

Add the apples and pears to the skillet cut side down. Cook for about 5 to 7 minutes until evenly caramelized, turning them several times. Carefully add a splash of Calvados, standing well back as the alcohol may flambé.

Pour in the apple juice and let bubble until the liquid has reduced and thickened to a syrupy sauce. Take off the heat and let cool slightly.

Divide the fruit among warm plates and spoon over the caramel sauce. Serve with a dollop of crème fraîche, if you like.

Quick flavor hits

Beyond the pepper mill, these are great flavor enhancers for quick meals:

Grated garlic   Save time chopping—instead grate peeled garlic cloves with a microplane or a small grater directly into the pan or bowl.

Curry salt   Mix 1 tsp (5ml) curry powder to 2 tsp (10ml) sea salt and use to add an extra kick to fish, shellfish, chicken, and pork. We often sprinkle a little curry salt onto fresh scallops in the restaurants.

Flavored oils   Brush a little chili, rosemary, or basil flavored oil on broiled vegetables or drizzle over pasta before serving to lift the flavor. Buy good quality flavored oils or make your own.

Flavored butter   Beat freshly chopped herbs and/or spices (crushed garlic, paprika, and saffron are my favorites) into softened salted butter, then roll in plastic wrap and chill or freeze. Cut slices as required and dot on piping hot meat, fish, or vegetables to pep up the flavor.

Herbed bread crumbs   Don't discard dry white bread. Cut off the crusts and whiz in a food processor with lots of herbs and some freshly grated Parmesan. Keep in the refrigerator or freezer and use as a tasty, colorful coating for fish fillets, lamb chops, or chicken breasts.

fast 5 salads

Salad of grilled asparagus & spinach
Minted melon, feta & fennel salad
Beet, goat cheese & apple salad
Italian leafy salad with walnut dressing
Tangerine, frisée & sweet potato salad

Salad of grilled asparagus & spinach

Serves 4

1lb (450g) asparagus, trimmed
5 tbsp (75ml) olive oil
sea salt and black pepper
4oz (125g) Roquefort or other blue cheese
1 tbsp (15ml) Dijon mustard
2 tbsp (30ml) cider vinegar
3 tbsp (45ml) walnut oil, plus extra
  to drizzle
7oz (200g) baby spinach leaves
½ cup (125ml) walnut halves, toasted

Peel the asparagus (lower part of the stems). Toss with 2 tbsp (30ml) olive oil and seasoning. Heat a griddle or stovetop grill pan until hot. Add the asparagus spears and cook for 8 minutes, turning occasionally, until tender. Set aside.

Crumble half the cheese into a large bowl and crush with a fork, mixing in 1–2 tbsp (15–30ml) water and the mustard to loosen it. Stir in the cider vinegar, then whisk in the walnut oil and the rest of the olive oil. Season with salt and pepper to taste. Toss through the spinach leaves and add a handful of toasted walnuts.

Pile the spinach onto four plates. Cut the grilled asparagus spears in two on the diagonal, if you like, and arrange on top of the spinach. Crumble over the remaining cheese and walnuts. Drizzle with a little more walnut oil to serve.

Minted melon, feta & fennel salad

Serves 4

2 large fennel bulbs, trimmed and tough
   outer leaves removed
1 Charentais (or ½ cantaloupe) melon
4oz (125g) mixed salad leaves
7oz (200g) feta cheese
handful of mint leaves, finely shredded

DRESSING:
2 tbsp (30ml) white wine vinegar
juice of ½ lemon
⅓ cup (75ml) olive oil
sea salt and black pepper

Slice the fennel as thinly as possible, using a mandolin if possible. Immerse in a bowl of iced water and set aside.

For the dressing, whisk together the wine vinegar, lemon juice, and olive oil, and season with salt and pepper to taste.

Halve the melon, seed, and peel, then slice into long wedges. Cut these across into thin slices.

Drain the fennel, pat dry with paper towels, and place in a salad bowl with the melon and salad leaves. Crumble over the feta. Add the shredded mint to the dressing and pour over the salad. Toss well and serve.

Beet, goat cheese & apple salad

Serves 4

1lb (450g) ready-cooked baby beets
1 Braeburn apple
squeeze of lemon juice
4oz (125g) goat cheese, crumbled
⅓ cup (75ml) toasted hazelnuts, coarsely
   chopped

VINAIGRETTE:
2 tbsp (30ml) balsamic vinegar
3 tbsp (45ml) hazelnut (or walnut) oil
3 tbsp (45ml) extra virgin olive oil
sea salt and black pepper

Whisk together the ingredients for the vinaigrette, seasoning with salt and pepper to taste.

Cut the baby beets into halves or quarters (wearing a pair of rubber gloves to avoid staining your hands). Quarter, core, and thinly slice the apple and toss with a little lemon juice to stop it discoloring.

Pile the beets and apple slices onto four plates and scatter over the goat cheese and hazelnuts. Drizzle with the vinaigrette and serve immediately.

Italian leafy salad with walnut dressing

Serves 4

2 heads of chicory, trimmed
1 small head of radicchio, trimmed
4oz (125g) wild arugula

DRESSING:
½ cup (125ml) walnut halves, toasted
1 large garlic clove, peeled and grated
grated zest and juice of 1 lemon
6–8 tbsp (90–120ml) extra virgin olive oil
sea salt and black pepper
2–3 tbsp (30–45ml) freshly grated
   Parmesan

Finely slice the chicory and radicchio and put into a large salad bowl with the arugula leaves.

For the dressing, coarsely grind the walnuts together with the garlic and lemon zest, using a large mortar and pestle. Stir in the lemon juice, olive oil, and seasoning to taste. Add the Parmesan and a little more olive oil or a splash of water, if you find the dressing is too thick.

Pour the dressing over the chicory, raddichio, and arugula. Toss well and serve.

Tangerine, frisée & sweet potato salad

Serves 4

2 large sweet potatoes, peeled
sea salt and black pepper
2 tangerines
olive oil, to brush
1–2 tbsp (15–30ml) orange or tangerine
   juice
¼ cup (50ml) Classic Vinaigrette (see
   page 248)
7oz (200g) frisée (curly endive)

Cut the sweet potatoes into ½-inch (1cm) thick circles and boil in a pan of salted water for 3 to 4 minutes until they are just tender when pierced with a small, dry knife. Meanwhile, peel and segment the tangerines, removing the white pith.

Drain the potatoes well and pat dry with paper towels. Heat a griddle or stovetop grill pan until hot. Grill the sweet potato slices in several batches: brush with olive oil, sprinkle with salt and pepper, then grill for 2 to 3 minutes on each side until charred.

For the dressing, whisk the orange or tangerine juice into the vinaigrette and check the seasoning.

Toss the frisée and tangerine segments with some of the dressing. Arrange on serving plates with the warm grilled potato slices. Trickle over the remaining dressing and serve.

Viva Italia!
{entertaining menu}

I love the Italian attitude to food—so long as you use the best and freshest ingredients, there is no need for complicated techniques or unnecessary frills. It is well exemplified in this menu. You might like to serve a leafy salad along with the main course, or to follow—as Italians would do. Serves 4.

planning your menu

Broiled sardines with gremolata
Veal piccata
Italian leafy salad (see page 66)
Easy tiramisu

- **Prepare the tiramisu and chill.**
- **Make the gremolata, prepare the sardines, and preheat the broiler.**
- **Assemble the ingredients for the veal piccata.**
- **Broil and serve the sardines.**
- **Cook the veal, make the creamy sauce, and serve.**
- **Follow with the salad (or serve alongside the main course).**
- **Top the tiramisu with a few sponge fingers and serve.**

BROILED SARDINES WITH GREMOLATA

" Zesty gremolata is the perfect foil for rich sardines. Like other oily fish, sardines spoil quickly so make sure they are very fresh when you buy them. Look for bright, clear eyes and firm flesh, and check that they smell faintly of the sea—definitely not of ammonia or too 'fishy'. **"**

Serves 4
8 very fresh sardines, cleaned
olive oil, to drizzle
handful of rosemary sprigs, leaves only
1 lemon, halved

GREMOLATA:
⅓ cup (75ml) olive oil
2 garlic cloves, peeled and finely grated
grated zest and juice of 1 lemon
handful of Italian parsley, chopped
sea salt and black pepper

To make the gremolata, mix the olive oil, garlic, lemon zest and juice, and chopped parsley together in a bowl. Season with salt and pepper to taste. Set aside.

Pat the sardines dry with paper towels and rub all over with a little olive oil. Lay them side by side in a robust roasting pan (or the broiler pan) and season with salt and pepper. Preheat the broiler to high.

Scatter the rosemary over the sardines and squeeze over some lemon juice. Broil for 4 to 5 minutes each side, basting the sardines with the pan juices as you turn them.

Transfer the sardines to a warm platter, spoon over the gremolata, and serve immediately.

VEAL PICCATA

" Young tender veal chops are fantastic served with a tangy, creamy sauce. Traditionally, the sauce for veal piccata consists simply of white wine and capers, but I find crème fraîche adds a lovely, velvety richness to the sauce. "

Serves 4

3 tbsp (45ml) olive oil

1 head of garlic (unpeeled), halved crosswise

4 veal chops, about 10oz (300g) each and 1–1¼ inches (2.5–3cm) thick

sea salt and black pepper

1 rosemary sprig

handful of thyme sprigs

generous ¾ cup (175ml) dry white wine

2 tbsp (30ml) capers, drained

⅓ cup (75ml) crème fraîche

Heat the olive oil
in a wide, heavy pan and add the garlic halves, cut side down. Allow the garlic to infuse the oil over medium-low heat for a minute, then increase the heat.

Season the veal chops
with salt and pepper and add to the pan. Throw in the herbs and pan-fry the veal for 1½ to 2 minutes on each side until golden brown. Remove the veal from the pan and let rest on a warm plate for 5 minutes.

Pour off the excess oil
from the pan, then add the wine, scraping the bottom to deglaze. Bring to a boil and let bubble until reduced by half, adding any juices from the meat.

Stir in the capers
and crème fraîche and simmer for a minute or two until the sauce is the desired consistency. Season generously with salt and pepper to taste. Remove and discard the garlic and herbs.

Spoon the sauce
onto four warm plates and place the veal chops on top. Serve immediately, with some country bread on the side for mopping up the delicious sauce.

EASY TIRAMISU

“ A good tiramisu makes a heavenly dessert but it is undoubtedly very rich and indulgent. For this quick, lighter version, light cream replaces eggs, though you can use whipping cream for a richer texture. **”**

Serves 4
⅔ cup (150ml) light cream
4 tbsp (60ml) confectioners' sugar
generous 1 cup (250ml) mascarpone
1 tsp (5ml) vanilla extract
3 tbsp (45ml) Marsala (or brandy or
 Tia Maria)
generous ¾ cup (175ml) strong coffee
 or espresso, cooled to room
 temperature
20–24 sponge fingers (savoiardi)
unsweetened cocoa powder, to dust

Whip the cream with 3 tbsp (45ml) confectioners' sugar until evenly blended, then beat in the mascarpone, vanilla extract, and 1 tbsp (15ml) Marsala.

Sweeten the coffee with the remaining 1 tbsp (15ml) confectioners' sugar, stir to dissolve, then add the rest of the Marsala.

Dip 4 sponge fingers in the coffee mixture and use them to line the base of four serving glasses (breaking them into shorter lengths if necessary to fit the glasses). Spoon or pipe over a layer of the mascarpone mixture. Repeat layering the dipped sponge fingers and mascarpone mix until you reach the top of the glasses.

Spoon the coffee mixture (leftover from dipping the sponge fingers) over the top and dust with sifted cocoa powder. Chill for at least 20 minutes.

Just before serving, stick two sponge fingers into each tiramisu.

77

5

sandwiches

Crayfish, avocado & mayo toasties
Pata negra, melon & mozzarella focaccia
Panini of pan-roasted vegetables
Fresh tuna open sandwich
Smoked salmon & cream cheese on rye

Crayfish, avocado & mayo toasties

Serves 4

Toss 14oz (400g) cooked crayfish tails with 4–5 tbsp (60–75ml) mayonnaise and ½ tsp (2ml) white truffle-infused olive oil. Stir through 1 chopped avocado and season with sea salt and black pepper to taste.

Lightly toast 4 thick slices of rustic white bread. Sandwich the crayfish filling between the toast slices and serve.

Pata negra, melon & mozzarella focaccia
Serves 4

Split 4 large pieces of focaccia (about 3 by 4 inches/8 by 10cm) in half. Place the bottom halves on plates and top with a few thin slices of ripe cantaloupe or Charentais melon.

Drape over a few slices of fresh buffalo mozzarella, 4 or 5 slices of pata negra ham, and a few basil leaves.

Drizzle lightly with extra virgin olive oil, sprinkle with a little sea salt, and grind over some black pepper. Sandwich together with the top focaccia halves and serve.

Panini of pan-roasted vegetables
Serves 4

Heat 3 tbsp (45ml) olive oil in a wide skillet. Cook 1 chopped red onion with a few thyme sprigs over high heat for 4 minutes or until it begins to soften. Tip in 1 chopped zucchini and 1 each chopped red and yellow bell pepper. Cook for a few minutes, stirring, until the vegetables are just tender. Season to taste.

Split 4 panini buns in half and spread both halves with pesto. Divide the vegetables among the bases and scatter over some shaved romano and a small handful of toasted pine nuts. Sandwich together with the panini tops.

Grill each sandwich in a panini press or toasted sandwich maker for a few minutes until compressed and warmed through.

TIP If you don't have a panini pan or toasted sandwich maker, wrap the paninis tightly in plastic wrap, weigh down with a heavy pan for a while, then unwrap and grill on both sides until warmed through.

Fresh tuna open sandwich

Serves 4

Season 2 thick tuna steaks and quickly sear in a very hot pan with a little olive oil, allowing 1½ to 2 minutes each side. Let cool slightly. Trim 1 or 2 baby romaine lettuce and separate the leaves. Toss in a bowl with a drizzle of olive oil and balsamic vinegar.

Toast 4 thick slices of crusty white bread and spread each with 1 tbsp (15ml) tapenade or pesto. Lay on plates and pile the lettuce leaves on top. Thickly slice the tuna steaks and arrange over the lettuce. Sprinkle with a little sea salt, black pepper, and olive oil, then serve.

Smoked salmon & cream cheese on rye

Serves 4

Season 7oz (200g) cream cheese with ½ tsp (2ml) cracked black pepper and a pinch of sea salt. Spread thickly onto 8 slices of rye bread. (Keep any remaining peppered cream cheese in the refrigerator for another sandwich.)

Lay 2 or 3 slices of smoked salmon on half of the bread slices, then top with a generous spoonful of caviar for a touch of luxury, if you like. Sandwich together with the rest of the bread slices and serve.

"Seasoning is especially important for fast dishes, which don't have long to develop a depth of flavor. I season a dish several times during cooking and always taste to check it at the end."

Fast fish
& fries
{everyday menu}

After Sunday roast and curry, fish and French fries must be the most popular British dish. Flounder, haddock, and cod are traditional, or you can buy cheaper, more sustainable fish—like hake, whiting, or pollack. Coat in bread crumbs and pan-fry, rather than deep-fry, for a healthy option and less cleaning up. Serves 4.

planning your menu

Pan-fried crumbed fish
        + Chunky fries   + Mushy peas
Strawberry shortbreads

- Preheat the oven.
- Cut the potatoes into French fries and parboil them.
- Prepare the cream mix for the strawberry shortbreads and chill.
- Make the mushy peas and leave in the pan for reheating.
- Drain the potatoes, toss with the oil and flavorings, and put into the oven.
- Coat the fish fillets, then pan-fry until crisp.
- Serve the fish with the fries and mushy peas.
- Assemble the shortbreads to serve.

PAN-FRIED CRUMBED FISH

What you eat with fish and French fries is a matter of personal taste. For me, it has to be a little malt vinegar and a generous sprinkling of salt, not forgetting a large mound of mushy peas on the side.

Serves 4

4 skinned white fish loin fillets
   (eg haddock, cod, or pollack), about
   6oz (175g) each
½ cup (125ml) all-purpose flour
sea salt and black pepper
1 large egg, beaten
1½ cups (375ml) fresh bread crumbs or
   Japanese panko bread crumbs (see tip)
3–4 tbsp (45–60ml) olive oil
lemon wedges, to serve

TIP Japanese panko bread crumbs are ideal to keep in the pantry to use as a fast substitute for fresh bread crumbs.

Check the fish fillets for any pin bones, removing any you find with a pair of tweezers.

Tip the flour onto a plate and season with salt and pepper, mixing well. Pour the beaten egg into a shallow dish. Scatter the bread crumbs on another plate.

Heat the olive oil in a large skillet. Dip the fish fillets into the seasoned flour to coat, shaking off excess. Dip into the beaten egg, and finally into the bread crumbs to coat evenly all over. Place in the hot skillet and pan-fry for about 5 minutes until golden and crisp all over, turning once.

Drain the fish on paper towels and serve immediately, with the chunky fries, mushy peas, and lemon wedges for squeezing.

Chunky fries

Heat the oven to 425°F (220°C) and place a sturdy roasting pan inside to heat up.

Cut the potatoes into ½-inch (1cm) thick French fries. Parboil in a pan of salted water for about 5 to 7 minutes until just tender when pierced with a skewer. Drain well and pat dry with a clean dish towel.

Tip the potatoes onto the hot roasting pan and scatter over the garlic and herbs. Drizzle generously with olive oil and sprinkle with salt and pepper. Toss the potatoes to coat in the oil and flavorings, using a pair of tongs.

Bake in the oven for 10 to 15 minutes until the fries are golden brown and crisp, turning them a few times. Drain on paper towels and serve immediately.

Serves 4
2¼lb (1kg) potatoes (eg round red), scrubbed or peeled
sea salt and black pepper
5 garlic cloves (unpeeled)
few thyme sprigs
few rosemary sprigs (leaves only)
olive oil, to drizzle

Mushy peas

Serves 4
2 x 10oz (284g) cans marrowfat peas
few pieces of butter
splash of white wine vinegar
sea salt and black pepper

Drain the peas, tip into a pan, and lightly crush with a fork or potato masher.

Place over medium heat and stir in the butter and a little splash of wine vinegar. Stir frequently for a few minutes until the peas are heated through. Season with salt and pepper to taste.

STRAWBERRY SHORTBREADS

" These can be ready in a matter of minutes and they look impressive—even thrown together in a higgledy-piggledy manner for a casual supper. Just make sure you buy fine quality, thin shortbreads and assemble just before serving. "

Serves 4

generous ¾ cup (175ml) crème fraîche

5 tbsp (75ml) whipping cream

2–3 tbsp (30–45ml) confectioners' sugar, plus extra to dust

8 all-butter round shortbreads

14oz (400g) strawberries, hulled and quartered

few mint sprigs (leaves only), roughly shredded, plus a few sprigs to finish

Put the crème fraîche, whipping cream, and 2 tbsp (30ml) confectioners' sugar into a large bowl. Beat lightly until smooth and just thick, taking care not to overwhisk. Taste and add a little more confectioners' sugar, if you like.

Place a shortbread on each serving plate. Spoon a large dollop of the creamy mixture on top. Scatter the strawberries and mint over the cream.

Dust the other shortbreads with confectioners' sugar and rest them on top of the strawberries. Add a mint sprig to each dessert and serve.

fast 5 eggs

Bacon, pea & goat cheese frittata
Poached duck egg with anchovy fingers
Scrambled eggs with crabmeat & chives
Baked egg florentine
Warm blood sausage & quail's egg salad

Bacon, pea & goat cheese frittata

Serves 4

1½ tbsp (22ml) butter
8 slices of smoked lean bacon, chopped
7oz (200g) peas (thawed, if frozen)
few basil leaves, roughly sliced or torn
8 large eggs, beaten
5oz (150g) goat cheese log with rind,
   thickly sliced
sea salt and black pepper
Parmesan, for grating
large handful of arugula leaves
2–3 tbsp (30–45ml) Classic Vinaigrette
   (see page 248)

Preheat the broiler to its highest setting. Melt the butter in a large nonstick skillet and cook the bacon until golden brown and crisp. Toss in the peas and cook for another minute or two, then add the basil.

Pour in the beaten eggs and gently shake the skillet over medium heat. As the frittata begins to set at the bottom, top with the goat cheese. Season generously with pepper and a little salt.

Grate some Parmesan over the frittata and place the pan under the hot broiler for a minute or two until the eggs are set on top. Slide onto a warm large plate.

Toss a handful of arugula leaves in vinaigrette to dress lightly, then pile on top of the frittata. Cut into wedges to serve.

Poached duck egg with anchovy fingers

Serves 4

4 very fresh duck eggs, at room temperature
1 tsp (5ml) white wine vinegar

ANCHOVY FINGERS:
2 tbsp (30ml) tapenade
4 slices of medium sliced white bread
about 16 salted anchovies in oil, drained
3–4 tbsp (45–60ml) olive oil

To be ready to poach the eggs, bring a wide, deep pan of water to a simmer and add the vinegar.

For the anchovy fingers, spread the tapenade on 2 slices of white bread and arrange the anchovies on top. Cover with the remaining bread slices, then flatten the sandwiches with a rolling pin and cut off the crusts. Heat the olive oil in a skillet and cook the anchovy sandwiches until golden brown on both sides. Remove and drain on paper towels, then slice into ½-inch (1cm) wide fingers; keep warm.

Crack the duck eggs, one at a time, into a teacup and slide them into the slowly simmering water. Poach for 2 to 3 minutes until the whites are set and the yolks are still runny in the middle. With a slotted spoon, carefully remove each one and place in a small warm bowl. Serve with the anchovy fingers, for dipping into the runny yolk.

Scrambled eggs with crabmeat & chives

Serves 4

2 tbsp (30ml) butter
12 large eggs, lightly beaten
7oz (200g) white (or mixture of white and brown) crabmeat, picked through
handful of chives, minced
sea salt and black pepper
2 tbsp (30ml) crème fraîche
4 thick slices of country bread, toasted

Melt the butter in a nonstick pan and add the beaten eggs. Stir with a wooden spoon over low heat for a few minutes until the eggs are half set but still quite runny.

Stir in the crabmeat, chives, and seasoning. Keep stirring until the eggs are just about to set, then quickly incorporate the crème fraîche and remove the pan from the heat.

Place a slice of toast on each warm plate and spoon the scrambled eggs on top. Serve immediately.

Baked egg florentine

2 tbsp (30ml) butter
1lb (450g) spinach leaves, washed and
  dried
sea salt and black pepper
4 large eggs, at room temperature
6–8 tbsp (90–120ml) crème fraîche
nutmeg, for grating

Heat the oven to 400°F (200°C). Melt the butter in a large pan over high heat. Add the spinach leaves and some seasoning and stir for a few seconds until the spinach has just wilted.

Divide the spinach among 4 buttered individual ceramic baking dishes and spread evenly, making a slight indentation in the center. Let cool slightly.

Crack an egg into each indentation, then carefully spoon the crème fraîche around. Season with a sprinkling of salt, pepper, and freshly grated nutmeg.

Bake in the oven for 10 to 12 minutes until the egg whites are set, but the yolks are still quite soft and runny in the center. Serve immediately.

Warm blood sausage & quail's egg salad

Serves 4

24 quail's eggs, at room temperature
7oz (200g) blood sausage
2–3 tbsp (30–45ml) olive oil
5 tbsp (75ml) Classic Vinaigrette (see page 248)
7oz (200g) mixed salad leaves
sea salt and black pepper

Bring a small pan of water to a gentle boil. Lower the quail's eggs into the water and cook for 2 minutes, then drain and refresh in a bowl of cold water. Peel off the shells and halve the eggs lengthwise, if you like.

Thickly slice the blood sausage into circles. Heat the olive oil in a nonstick skillet and pan-fry the sausage slices for 2 to 3 minutes on each side. Add the quail's eggs to the skillet to warm through briefly. Pour in the vinaigrette and quickly remove the skillet from the heat.

Tip the skillet contents into a large bowl containing the salad leaves. Toss lightly and season with a little salt and pepper. Pile onto individual plates to serve.

Outdoor eating
{entertaining menu}

There is nothing like sharing an alfresco meal with family and friends, either on a picnic blanket in a grassy meadow or just out in the back yard. The dishes on this menu are ideal for summer eating. The choice is yours whether you take them on a picnic or simply into the back yard. Serves 4.

Tomato & pesto tart
Peppered lamb steaks
+ Green bean, red onion & romano salad
Macerated summer berries with clotted cream
Fresh lemonade

- Preheat the oven. Make the tart and put in the oven to bake.
- Blanch the green beans and salt the onion for the salad.
- Macerate the summer berries.
- Make the lemonade.
- Finish the salad.
- Pan-fry the lamb steaks (and cool if taking on a picnic).
- Pack everything in containers to take on a picnic or arrange on platters to eat in the back yard, leaving the dessert in the refrigerator until ready to serve.

TOMATO & PESTO TART

> " To me, this tart—with its filling of vine-ripened tomatoes set against a background of fresh basil pesto—epitomizes summer. For a different dimension, use walnuts in the pesto instead of pine nuts. The tart travels well if you're planning a picnic and it's delicious warm or cold. "

Serves 4

9oz (250g) puff pastry

all-purpose flour, to dust

1 egg yolk, beaten with 1 tbsp (15ml) water, to glaze

2–3 tbsp (30–45ml) pesto (see page 249)

4oz (125g) cherry tomatoes, halved

1 small rosemary sprig (leaves only), minced

few thyme sprigs (leaves only)

2 green onions, trimmed and finely sliced

2 tbsp (30ml) freshly grated Parmesan

3–4 basil leaves, roughly chopped

olive oil, to drizzle

Heat the oven to 425°F (220°C). Roll out the puff pastry on a lightly floured counter to a large rectangle, about 6 by 10 inches (15 by 25cm). Using a sharp knife, score a ½-inch (1cm) border around the edge, making sure you don't cut right through the pastry. Brush the border with egg glaze.

Spread the pesto over the pastry (within the border) and arrange the tomato halves on top. Scatter over the chopped rosemary and thyme, green onions, and grated Parmesan.

Bake for 20 minutes until the pastry is golden brown and crisp. Scatter over the chopped basil and drizzle with a little olive oil. Serve the tart warm or cold, cut into quarters.

PEPPERED LAMB STEAKS

"If you are eating in the back yard, I suggest you serve the lamb still warm. Otherwise, for a picnic, take the cooked steaks with you; slice them thickly and scatter on top of the salad before applying the dressing."

Serves 4

2 tbsp (30ml) black peppercorns
4 lamb leg steaks, each 9oz (250g) and about ¾ inch (2cm) thick
2 tbsp (30ml) olive oil

Crush the peppercorns lightly, using a mortar and pestle, then tip into a strainer and shake to get rid of the fine dust. Tip the crushed peppercorns onto a plate and press both sides of the steaks onto the peppercorns to coat.

Heat the olive oil in a large skillet. Add the lamb steaks and pan-fry over high heat for 2 to 3 minutes on each side. Remove from the skillet and let rest for 5 minutes.

Slice the peppered lamb thickly and serve alongside (or on top of) the salad. Serve warm or cold, with crusty bread.

Green bean, red onion & romano salad

Add the beans to a pan of boiling salted water and cook for 4 minutes or until just tender. Drain, refresh in cold water, then pat dry with paper towels.

Put the onion in a colander, sprinkle with salt, and leave for 5 minutes. Holding the colander over the sink, pour on a kettleful of boiling water to remove some of the onion's acidity. Drain well and pat dry.

Toss the beans, onion, and romano together in a bowl. For the dressing, whisk together the olive oil, lemon juice, and salt and pepper to taste (or shake to emulsify in a screw-topped jar).

Drizzle the dressing over the salad to serve.

Serves 4

14oz (400g) green beans, trimmed
sea salt and black pepper
1 red onion, peeled and thinly sliced
2oz (50g) romano, freshly grated
2–3 tbsp (30–45ml) extra virgin olive oil
juice of ½ lemon

MACERATED SUMMER BERRIES
WITH CLOTTED CREAM

" This is my idea of summer in a bowl. Clotted cream is the ultimate indulgence, but you might prefer a scoop of vanilla ice cream or a dollop of crème fraîche. "

Serves 4

7oz (200g) strawberries, hulled and quartered if large

1lb (450g) other mixed berries (eg raspberries, red currants, and blackberries)

2 tbsp (30ml) confectioners' sugar

⅔ cup (150ml) Muscat (or other sweet dessert wine)

clotted cream (Devonshire cream) or thick cream, to serve

Toss all of the berries together in a bowl with the confectioners' sugar and Muscat. Cover and let macerate in the refrigerator for 15 to 20 minutes.

Divide the berries among individual bowls, spoon over the liquor, and serve with a dollop of clotted cream.

Fresh lemonade

Squeeze the juice from the lemons and limes and strain into a large pitcher. Tip in the sugar and stir well to dissolve. Put the spent citrus skins into the pitcher with the basil and fill with ice cubes. Top off with cold water to taste.

Serves 4

2 lemons, halved

2 limes, halved

½ cup (125ml) superfine sugar

few basil sprigs

plenty of ice cubes

"Don't skip meals or resort to junk food, however busy you are. Keep some great standby ingredients in the refrigerator and freezer and you'll always be able to run up a speedy, nourishing working lunch."

fast
5
working lunches

Pastrami & cream cheese bagel
Fusilli salad with merguez & olives
Leftover roast chicken salad
Rice noodle & smoked mackerel salad
Sausage & beans

Pastrami & cream cheese bagel

Serves 2

Split 2 poppyseed bagels in half. Lightly toast them if you're preparing lunch to eat straightaway.

Mix 3½oz (100g) cream cheese with 1 tbsp (15ml) whole grain mustard and salt and pepper to taste. Spread evenly over the cut surfaces of the bagel halves.

Arrange 2 or 3 pastrami slices, a sliced large gherkin, and a small handful of arugula leaves on each bagel base. Sandwich together with the bagel tops.

Fusilli salad with merguez & olives

Serves 2

Cook 5oz (150g) fusilli in a pan of well salted water for 10 to 12 minutes or until al dente.

In the meantime, thinly slice 7oz (200g) merguez sausages on the diagonal. Heat 2 tbsp (30ml) olive oil in a skillet and cook the sausage slices over medium heat until golden brown. Toss through ¼ cup (50ml) sun-dried tomatoes and ½ cup (125ml) quartered pitted olives. Warm through for a minute or two, then take off the heat.

Drain the pasta and toss with the sausage mix. Taste and adjust the seasoning. Stir through a handful of chopped mixed herbs, such as Italian parsley, chives, and basil. Serve warm or cold.

Leftover roast chicken salad

Serves 2

Trim 7oz (200g) watercress, removing the stalks, then wash and dry well on paper towels. Slice or shred the meat from ½ roast chicken (perhaps left over from yesterday's roast).

For the dressing, mix the juice of ½ lemon with 6 tbsp (90ml) extra virgin olive oil, adding any pan juices from the roast chicken and salt and pepper to taste. Toss the chicken in the dressing.

Add the watercress to the chicken just before serving and toss to mix. Serve with lemon wedges on the side and a few chunks of crusty baguette.

TIP If you're taking the salad to work, pack the watercress and chicken in separate containers and toss together at lunchtime.

Rice noodle & smoked mackerel salad
Serves 2

Put a 2½oz (75g) bundle of rice noodles into a large bowl, pour over boiling water to cover, and let soak for 10 minutes. Blanch 4oz (125g) trimmed sugar snap peas in a pan of salted water for 2 minutes until still slightly crunchy. Drain and refresh under cold running water, then slice in half, if you like.

Mix the juice of ½ lime with 1 tbsp (15ml) each light soy sauce, fish sauce, mirin, sesame oil, and grated fresh ginger. Drain the noodles well, then toss with the sugar snaps and dressing.

Flake 4oz (125g) hot-smoked mackerel (coated in peppercorns) into large pieces and scatter over the dressed rice noodles and sugar snaps. Sprinkle with 2 tbsp (30ml) toasted sesame seeds and a finely sliced green onion. Serve cold.

Sausage & beans
Serves 2

Pan-fry 4 Toulouse sausages in a wide, heavy pan with 2 tbsp (30ml) olive oil and a few thyme sprigs. Add 2 finely sliced garlic cloves and cook for 3 to 4 minutes, stirring occasionally, until the sausages are golden brown.

Tip in a 14oz (398g) can mixed beans (drained and rinsed), then a 14oz (398g) can chopped tomatoes. Bring to a simmer, partially cover, and stew for 10 to 12 minutes, by which time the sausages should be cooked through.

TIP Prepare ahead, cool, and pack in a rigid plastic container. Reheat in the microwave at work or in a pan over low heat.

Season with salt, pepper, and a pinch of sugar if the tomato sauce is too sharp. Serve in bowls with chunks of crusty bread.

115

Mexican flavors
{everyday menu}

Fajitas are fantastic for a casual midweek meal that you can eat with your hands. Get everyone involved in making them: someone to slice the peppers and beef; another to make the guacamole; and a third to prepare the dessert. Supper will be ready in no time. Serves 4.

planning your menu

Beef fajitas with sour cream & guacamole
Melon with tequila & lime

- Prepare the melon and steep in the tequila lime dressing in the refrigerator.
- Put four serving glasses in the refrigerator to chill.
- Slice the beef and peppers and toss them with the spice mix.
- Make the guacamole and set aside.
- Cook the beef and peppers and warm up the tortillas.
- Assemble the fajitas and serve.
- Divide the melon among glasses, top with lime zest and mint, then serve.

BEEF FAJITAS
WITH SOUR CREAM & GUACAMOLE

“ The spice mix I use here for the beef and peppers is quite fiery, but you can easily tone it down if you're catering for young children who can't take the heat. Simply replace the chili powder with ground coriander. ”

Serves 4

1⅓lb (600g) beef tenderloin
1 red bell pepper
2 yellow bell peppers
1 tsp (5ml) ground cumin
½ tsp (2ml) hot (or medium) chili powder
½ tsp (2ml) paprika
sea salt and black pepper
3 tbsp (45ml) olive oil
6–8 plain tortillas
6–8 tbsp (90–120ml) sour cream
few cilantro sprigs (leaves only),
   roughly torn

GUACAMOLE:
2 medium ripe avocados
juice of 1 lime
1 garlic clove, peeled and finely grated
½ red chile, seeded and minced
1 shallot, peeled and minced
2 ripe plum tomatoes, minced
handful of cilantro (leaves only),
   chopped

TIP Make up a quantity of spice mix and keep in a sealed jar, ready to use for fajitas or a spicy stir-fry whenever you fancy.

Slice the beef into long, thin strips and place in a bowl. Halve, core, and seed the bell peppers, then cut into strips.

In a small jar, mix together the cumin, chili powder, paprika, salt, and pepper. Add half the spice mix to the beef strips and mix well. Add the rest to the sliced peppers and toss to coat. Set aside to marinate.

To make the guacamole, halve the avocados and remove the pits. Scoop the flesh into a bowl, add the lime juice, and lightly mash with a fork until you get a chunky paste. Add the garlic, chile, shallot, tomatoes, and cilantro. Mix well and season with salt and pepper to taste. Set aside.

Heat a large wok and add the olive oil. When it is very hot, tip in the bell peppers and sauté until they are slightly soft, then toss in the beef strips. Cook for 2 minutes, stirring and tossing frequently, until the beef is just cooked. Remove from the wok and keep warm.

Warm up the tortillas in a dry skillet for about 10 seconds on each side. Put some beef and bell peppers along the center of each tortilla and add a dollop of sour cream and some guacamole. Scatter over some torn cilantro and roll up. Serve immediately.

MELON WITH TEQUILA & LIME

" Fragrant honeydew melon tossed in a tequila, honey, and lime dressing is the perfect refreshing dessert after a meal of spicy fajitas. If you don't possess a melon baller, simply cut the melon into thin slices and drizzle with the dressing. "

Serves 4

1 honeydew melon, preferably chilled
2–3 tbsp (30–45ml) cold tequila
**finely grated zest of ½ lime, plus extra
    to serve**
juice of ½ lime
2–3 tbsp (30–45ml) runny honey
tiny pinch of fine sea salt
few mint sprigs (leaves only), chopped

Halve the melon and remove the seeds with a spoon. Using a melon baller, scoop the flesh into neat balls and place in a large bowl.

Mix the tequila, lime zest and juice, honey, and salt together in a small pitcher. Taste and add a little more honey if the dressing is too sour. Pour over the melon balls, toss gently to mix, and chill for at least 10 to 15 minutes.

Divide the melon balls among serving glasses, grate over some lime zest, and sprinkle with freshly chopped mint to serve.

*f*ast pasta 5

Spaghetti with anchovy, garlic & parsley
Pappardelle, smoked trout & tomatoes
Linguine with tomatoes, olives & capers
Penne, green beans & goat cheese
Pasta with pancetta, leek & mushrooms

Spaghetti with anchovy, garlic & parsley

Serves 4

10oz (300g) dried spaghetti
sea salt and black pepper
3 tbsp (45ml) olive oil, plus extra
  to drizzle
2 garlic cloves, peeled and thinly sliced
6oz (175g) marinated anchovies, roughly
  chopped
bunch of Italian parsley, roughly
  chopped
freshly grated Parmesan, to serve

Cook the spaghetti in boiling salted water for 8 to 10 minutes or until al dente.

Heat the olive oil in a large pan, in the meantime. Add the garlic and cook over medium heat until golden brown at the edges. Stir in the chopped anchovies.

Drain the spaghetti and tip into the pan with the garlic and anchovies. Add the chopped parsley and season to taste with salt and pepper. Toss well.

Divide among warm bowls and serve with grated Parmesan and a drizzle of olive oil.

Pappardelle, smoked trout & tomatoes

Serves 4

6 vine-ripened plum tomatoes

sea salt and black pepper

15 semi-dried tomatoes in oil (about 3¼oz/95g)

2 garlic cloves, peeled and roughly chopped

2 banana shallots (or 4 regular ones), peeled and roughly chopped

¾ cup (175ml) olive oil

juice of ½ lemon

1lb 2oz (500g) fresh pappardelle or tagliatelle

1⅓lb (600g) skinless smoked trout fillets, flaked into large chunks

Parmesan, for grating

Add the plum tomatoes
to a large pan of boiling salted water and blanch for 2 minutes. Lift out with a slotted spoon to a bowl of iced water to cool for a few minutes, then remove and peel off the skins. Halve the tomatoes and squeeze out the seeds.

Put the tomatoes
into a food processor along with the semi-dried tomatoes, garlic, shallots, olive oil, and lemon juice. Whiz to a smooth sauce and season with salt and pepper to taste. Pour the sauce into a pan and warm through over medium-high heat while you cook the pasta.

Cook the pasta
in boiling salted water (the pan you used for the tomatoes) for 2 minutes until al dente. Drain well, then toss with the tomato dressing and flaked trout. Divide among warm plates and grate over some Parmesan to serve.

Linguine with tomatoes, olives & capers

Serves 4

10oz (300g) dried linguine or spaghetti

sea salt and black pepper

3 tbsp (45ml) olive oil, plus extra to drizzle

2 large garlic cloves, peeled and minced

1 large red onion, peeled and chopped

1 red chile, seeded and finely sliced

6–8 anchovies in oil, drained and minced

1¼ cups (300ml) pitted black olives, quartered or chopped

3 tbsp (45ml) capers, rinsed and drained

9oz (250g) cherry tomatoes, halved

handful of basil leaves, shredded

Add the pasta
to a pot of boiling salted water and cook for 8 to 10 minutes or until al dente.

Meanwhile,
heat the olive oil in a wide pan and sauté the garlic, onion, chile, and anchovies for 1 to 2 minutes. Add the olives, capers, and tomatoes, and stir over high heat for a few more minutes until the onions are soft.

Drain the pasta
and toss with the sauce and shredded basil. Taste and adjust the seasoning (salt probably won't be needed because the anchovies, capers, and olives are quite salty).

Divide among warm bowls
and drizzle over a little more olive oil, if you wish, before serving.

Penne, green beans & goat cheese

Serves 4

10oz (300g) dried penne (or other pasta
   shapes)
sea salt and black pepper
6 tbsp (90ml) butter
1 red chile, trimmed, seeded, and minced
few rosemary sprigs (leaves only),
   chopped
9oz (250g) Kentucky wonder beans,
   trimmed and sliced on the diagonal
extra virgin olive oil, to drizzle
5oz (150g) soft rindless goat cheese log
⅓ cup (75ml) toasted pine nuts

Add the pasta to a large pan of boiling salted water and
cook until al dente, about 8 to 10 minutes.

Meanwhile, melt the butter in a large pan, add the chile
and rosemary and warm over low heat for 1 to 2 minutes to let the
flavors infuse. Turn up the heat, add the beans, and cook for 3 to
4 minutes, stirring occasionally, until they are tender.

Drain the pasta and toss with a little olive oil, then mix
with the beans. Off the heat, crumble in the cheese and toss to mix,
adding a splash of boiling water if the sauce is too thick. Season with
salt and pepper to taste, scatter over the pine nuts, and serve.

Pasta with pancetta, leek & mushrooms

Serves 4

10oz (300g) dried pasta shells
   (conchiglie)
sea salt and black pepper
3–4 tbsp (45–60ml) olive oil
4½oz (135g) pancetta, sliced
2 medium leeks, trimmed and finely
   sliced
9oz (250g) cremini mushrooms, trimmed
   and sliced
2–3 tbsp (30–45ml) crème fraîche
bunch of Italian parsley, chopped

Add the pasta shells to a pot of boiling salted
water and cook for 8 to 10 minutes or until al dente.

Meanwhile, heat the olive oil in a large skillet and add the
pancetta. Cook for a few minutes until golden brown, then add the
leeks, mushrooms, and a little salt and pepper. Stir over high heat for
6 to 8 minutes until the leeks are tender.

Drain the pasta and immediately toss with the leeks,
pancetta, and mushrooms, and the crème fraîche. Season with salt
and pepper to taste. Scatter over the chopped parsley to serve.

"For me, cooking and eating seasonally is a joy. Homegrown foods at their peak of perfection are best prepared simply with the minimum of cooking."

Easy for a crowd
{everyday menu}

Cooking for a larger number needn't be time-consuming. The secret is to keep things simple. If you possibly can, prepare some of the food in advance—make the ragout and/or the cheesecake up to a day ahead, or at least chop up the vegetables well in advance. Serves 8.

Baked chicken with eggplant, zucchini
& tomato ragout
No-bake berry cheesecake

- Preheat the oven. Prepare and chop the vegetables for the ragout.
- Make the cookie topping for the dessert and chill.
- Line 8 ramekins with plastic wrap for the cheesecakes.
- Whip up the creamy cheese filling, fill the ramekins, and chill.
- Season and sear the chicken breasts, then set aside.
- Cook the vegetables in the pan.
- Put the chicken and vegetables into the oven.
- Soften the blueberries and let cool.
- Rest the chicken, then serve the main course.
- Unmold the cheesecakes, add the topping and berries, then serve.

BAKED CHICKEN
WITH EGGPLANT, ZUCCHINI & TOMATO RAGOUT

"" Chicken breasts are quickly seared, then baked on Mediterranean vegetables for a great one-pot dish. For convenience, you can make the ragout well in advance, but for best results, bake the chicken breasts just before serving. ""

Serves 8

5 tbsp (75ml) olive oil, plus extra to oil

8 large skinless chicken breasts

sea salt and black pepper

4 banana shallots, peeled and roughly chopped

4 garlic cloves (unpeeled), smashed

2 medium eggplants, trimmed and chopped

handful of thyme sprigs

handful of rosemary sprigs

4 zucchini, trimmed and chopped

glass of dry white wine

8 plum tomatoes, peeled, seeded, and chopped, or 14oz (398g) canned chopped tomatoes

Heat the oven to 375°F (190°C). Heat a large heavy skillet and add 3 tbsp (45ml) olive oil. Season the chicken breasts with salt and pepper.

Sear the chicken in batches: cook skinned side down for 3 to 4 minutes until golden brown, then turn over and cook the other side for 2 to 3 minutes. Transfer to a plate.

Add the remaining oil to the skillet and tip in the shallots, garlic, eggplants, and a few thyme and rosemary sprigs. Cook for 5 to 7 minutes, stirring occasionally, until the onions are soft and translucent, and the eggplants are starting to soften. Season generously with salt and pepper.

Add the zucchini, then pour in the wine and simmer until it has reduced by half. In the meantime, put an oiled large roasting pan in the oven to warm up.

Stir the tomatoes through the vegetables and tip into the roasting pan. Place the seared chicken breasts on top and scatter over some more herb sprigs. Bake in the oven for 5 to 10 minutes, depending on the thickness of the chicken, until firm and cooked through.

Rest for 5 minutes before serving on warm plates, with plenty of crusty bread on the side.

NO-BAKE
BERRY CHEESECAKE

" To be contrary, I've inverted the classic components of a cheesecake, topping the vanilla cream cheese with a cookie topping and serving glazed blueberries on the side. If you haven't time to shape individual cheesecakes in ramekins, just layer the vanilla cream cheese and blueberries in glasses and scatter the crumb mix on top. "

Serves 8
TOPPING:
8 graham crackers
6 tbsp (90ml) superfinesugar
½ cup (125ml) unsalted butter

BERRIES:
10oz (300g) blueberries (or
  blackberries)
2 tbsp (30ml) superfine sugar
splash of crème de cassis or water

VANILLA CREAM CHEESE:
14oz (400g) cream cheese
6 tbsp (90ml) confectioners' sugar
juice of ½ lemon
1 vanilla bean, split
2¼ cups (575ml) whipping cream

TO FINISH:
confectioners' sugar, to dust

For the topping, coarsely grind the crackers in a food processor. Melt the sugar in a heavy nonstick pan until it begins to caramelize, then carefully add the butter, shaking the pan to mix the caramel with the butter as it melts. Add the crushed crackers and toss to coat in the caramel. Tip onto a plate, chill for 5 minutes until firm, then break into pieces. Wipe out the pan with paper towels.

Tip the blueberries into the pan and sprinkle with the 2 tbsp sugar (30ml) and a splash of cassis or water. Cook over medium-high heat for a minute until the blueberries are slightly soft. Spread out on a plate and let cool.

For the vanilla cream cheese, put the cream cheese, confectioners' sugar, and lemon juice in a large bowl. Add the seeds from the vanilla bean and beat until smooth. In another bowl, lightly whip the cream until it forms soft peaks, then fold into the cream cheese mixture.

To shape individual cheesecakes, line 8 ramekins with plastic wrap. Fill with the cream cheese mixture and level the tops with the back of a knife. Chill until ready to serve.

Turn out the cheesecakes onto serving plates and remove the plastic wrap. Scatter the topping over the cheesecakes and spoon the blueberries around the plate. Dust with confectioners' sugar and serve immediately.

fast 5 shellfish

Mussels in an aromatic coconut broth

Serves 4

3 tbsp (45ml) olive oil
4½lb (2kg) fresh mussels, scrubbed
   clean (beards removed)
2 garlic cloves (unpeeled), halved
few thyme sprigs
½ cup (100ml) dry white wine
14oz (398ml) can coconut milk
1 lemon grass stalk, halved lengthwise
1 red chile, thinly sliced on the diagonal
2 green onions, trimmed and finely
   sliced on the diagonal
sea salt and black pepper
cilantro leaves, to finish

Heat a large heavy pan with a tight-fitting lid until it is very hot, then add the olive oil. Quickly tip in the mussels, garlic, thyme, and wine. Cover the pan with the lid and let the mussels steam for 3 to 4 minutes until they are fully opened.

Drain the mussels over a bowl to catch the liquor, then pour it into a clean pan and boil to reduce by half. Add the coconut milk, lemon grass, chile, green onions, and seasoning. Bring to a simmer and let bubble for 2 minutes.

Meanwhile, discard any unopened mussels and the garlic, then divide the mussels among warm serving bowls. Ladle the hot coconut broth over the mussels, picking out and discarding the lemon grass. Scatter over some cilantro leaves to serve.

Crab spring rolls

Serves 4

8 large spring roll wrappers (about
  10 inch/25cm square)
1 large egg white, for brushing
peanut oil, for deep-frying
sweet chili sauce (see page 249),
  for dipping

FILLING:
9oz (250g) white crabmeat
2 green onions, trimmed and finely
  sliced
small handful of cilantro leaves,
  chopped
1 tbsp (15ml) whole grain mustard
1½ tbsp (22ml) mayonnaise
sea salt and black pepper
tiny squeeze of lime juice

TIP Spring roll wrappers are
easy to use. Most Asian food stores and
some supermarkets now stock them.

For the filling, toss all the ingredients together in a bowl until evenly combined, adding salt, pepper, and lime juice to taste.

Lay a spring roll wrapper on a board with a corner facing you. (Keep the rest covered with a dish towel to prevent them drying out.) Spoon 2 tbsp (30ml) of the crabmeat filling onto the bottom of the wrapper (as shown), then brush the surrounding pastry with egg white. Fold the bottom edge up over the filling, brush the sides with egg white, and fold them in and over the filling, like an envelope. Roll up into a log. Repeat with the rest of the wrappers and filling.

Heat the oil for deep-frying (at least a 2½-inch/6cm depth) in a suitable pan to 350°F (180°C). To check the oil is hot enough, drop in a cube of bread—it should sizzle vigorously. Deep-fry the rolls in batches for 40 to 50 seconds until golden brown and crisp. Drain on paper towels.

Cut the spring rolls in half on the diagonal and serve warm, with a bowl of sweet chili sauce on the side for dipping.

Oyster shooters

Serves 4

¼ cup (50ml) tomato juice, chilled
squeeze of lemon juice
generous dash of Worcestershire sauce
generous dash of hot pepper sauce
2 shots (about ¼ cup/50ml) cold vodka
4 fresh oysters
sea salt and black pepper
celery salt, for dipping (optional)
squeeze of lime juice (optional)

In a small pitcher, mix together the tomato juice, lemon juice, Worcestershire sauce, hot pepper sauce, and vodka. Shuck the oysters and add the juices to the tomato mixture. Season with salt and pepper to taste. Tip some celery salt into a bowl, if using.

Wet the rims of four shot glasses with a little water or lime juice, then dip in the celery salt to coat, if you like. Carefully pour the tomato mixture into the glasses to three-quarters fill them. Drop an oyster into each glass and serve immediately.

TIP To shuck an oyster, hold in a folded dish towel and insert an oyster knife through the hinge of the shell. Keeping the oyster level, wriggle the knife to sever the hinge muscle, then push it in a bit further and twist up to lift the top shell. Tip the juice into a bowl and remove any pieces of shell from the oyster. Slide the knife along the bottom shell to release the oyster.

Easy lobster thermidor
Serves 4

2 freshly cooked lobsters
Parmesan, for grating
small handful of chives and chervil,
chopped

SAUCE:
⅓ cup (75ml) crème fraîche
2 egg yolks
1 tsp (5ml) dry English mustard
sea salt and black pepper

Uncurl the lobster tails and place them flat on a board. Using a strong pair of kitchen scissors, snip along the bottom shells, then use a large knife to cut the tails into two halves. Remove the flesh and place back into the shells, the other way around.

To prepare the claws, pull out the small claw to release the blade, then crack open the shells of the thick claws with the back of a knife. Gently pull out the flesh and place on a baking sheet, along with the lobster tails.

Heat the broiler to its highest setting. Mix the sauce ingredients together, then spoon over the lobster tails and claws. Grate over a little Parmesan and broil for 3 to 4 minutes until golden brown on top. Serve immediately, with a sprinkling of chopped herbs.

141

Shrimp with orange & tequila

Serves 4

3 tbsp (45ml) olive oil
14oz (400g) fresh jumbo shrimp
2 garlic cloves, peeled and finely sliced
sea salt and black pepper
generous splash of tequila
juice of 1 orange, or 2 clementines

Heat a large skillet, then add the olive oil. When hot, add the shrimp with the garlic and some seasoning. Pan-fry for 2 minutes on each side until the shrimp turn bright red and opaque.

Add a splash of tequila, carefully and standing well back as it may flambé. Pour in the orange juice and let bubble for a few minutes until the liquid has reduced. Transfer to a warm plate and serve immediately.

"However amazing a dish looks, it is always the taste that lingers in your memory. Family and friends will appreciate a meal that tastes superb—even if you've brought the pan to the table."

tapas spread
{entertaining menu}

Feasting on a selection of smaller dishes is popular in many parts of the world—Chinese dim sum, Middle Eastern mezze, and Spanish tapas are all examples. This menu is based on some of my favorite tapas. They are all quick to make and you can add bowls of Spanish olives and salted Marcona almonds to extend the spread. Serves 4.

Fried chorizo with parsley
Sautéed shrimp with green peppercorns
Manchego & membrillo on olive bread
Iberian ham with garlic & chickpeas
Squid with olives

- Assemble the manchego tapas. Arrange on a platter and keep covered.
- Cook the chorizo and toss with the parsley; keep warm.
- Pan-fry the garlic and chickpeas; keep warm.
- Cook the squid and olives.
- Sauté the shrimp with paprika and green peppercorns.
- Assemble the ham, garlic, and chickpeas on a platter.
- Plate the other tapas in warm bowls to serve.

146

FRIED CHORIZO WITH PARSLEY

66 If you can, buy fresh chorizo from a good butcher or deli for this dish. Serve the fried chorizo as it is, or pile onto crusty bread slices and drizzle with the orange-colored oil from the pan. **99**

Serves 4
9oz (250g) chorizo sausage
2 tbsp (30ml) olive oil
squeeze of lemon juice
handful of Italian parsley (leaves only),
   roughly chopped

Peel away the skin from the chorizo, then chop the sausage into bite-size chunks.

Heat the olive oil in a skillet. Add the chorizo and pan-fry, tossing frequently, over high heat for 2 minutes or until it has released its oils and is browned at the edges.

Add the lemon juice and stir in the chopped parsley. Serve warm.

SAUTEED SHRIMP
WITH GREEN PEPPERCORNS

66 Paprika and green peppercorns give shrimp a vibrant piquancy. I like to use Madagascar green peppercorns (usually sold brined in small cans) for their slightly spicy, tangy flavor. Buy good quality cooked shrimp in the shell. **99**

Heat the olive oil in a large skillet until hot. Pat the shrimp dry, then tip into the pan. Sprinkle with the paprika, add a pinch of salt, and sauté for 1 minute, tossing occasionally.

Add the peppercorns and lemon juice to the skillet and sauté for another 30 seconds. Transfer the shrimp to a bowl and serve warm.

Serves 4
1 tbsp (15ml) olive oil
7oz (200g) cooked shrimp in the
   shell
½ tsp paprika
sea salt
1–2 tbsp (15–30ml) green
   peppercorns, drained
juice of ½ lemon

MANCHEGO & MEMBRILLO
ON OLIVE BREAD

" I love the combination of salty cheese and sweet membrillo in this classic tapa. Membrillo, a Spanish-style quince jelly, is increasingly easy to find in good delis and supermarkets. You can buy it in blocks that you slice, or in softer pastes that can be spread on toasts. Similarly, manchego cheese is relatively easy to obtain. **"**

Serves 4

4 thin slices of olive bread
5oz (150g) manchego cheese
8 tsp (40ml) membrillo paste
extra virgin olive oil, to drizzle
sea salt and black pepper

TIP Try other toppings to add variety to your tapas spread, such as jamon and piquillo peppers, or marinated anchovies and sliced manzanilla olives.

Cut each slice of bread into four. Cut the manchego cheese into medium slices and remove any outer rind.

Place a slice of cheese on each bread slice and top with a spoonful of membrillo paste. (If using firm membrillo, cut into thin slices and place on top of the cheese.)

Drizzle with a little olive oil and sprinkle with sea salt and a grinding of black pepper. Arrange the tapas on a serving platter.

IBERIAN HAM WITH GARLIC & CHICKPEAS

" It is quite common to pair savory Iberian ham with beans in Spain. This recipe uses chickpeas but you could substitute canned cooked cannellini, flageolet, or cranberry beans, whichever you have to hand. "

Serves 4

2 tbsp (30ml) olive oil

2 garlic cloves, peeled and thinly sliced

4oz (125g) canned chickpeas, drained and rinsed

sea salt and black pepper

8 slices Iberian ham

Heat the olive oil in a skillet over low heat. Add the garlic slices and cook for a minute to allow the flavors to infuse. Tip in the chickpeas, increase the heat to medium, and season with salt and pepper to taste. Warm through, stirring occasionally, then take the skillet off the heat.

Drape the ham slices on a serving platter and spoon over the chickpeas, garlic, and oil from the skillet. Serve warm.

SQUID WITH OLIVES

" This is a wonderfully simple way to cook baby squid. The vinaigrette imparts a zesty flavor and helps to tenderize the squid. "

Serves 4

9oz (250g) baby squid (about 6–8), cleaned

¼ cup (50ml) black olives

¼ cup (50ml) extra virgin olive oil

¼ cup (50ml) peanut oil

juice of ½ lemon

sea salt and black pepper

small handful of Italian parsley, roughly chopped

Rinse the squid and pat dry. Slice the body into thin rings and place these in a pan with the tentacles.

Add the olives, oils, lemon juice, and seasoning. Slowly bring the liquid to a boil, then immediately turn off the heat. Cover and let the squid cook in the residual heat of the vinaigrette. The squid is ready when it turns white and opaque.

Stir the chopped parsley through the squid, then, with a slotted spoon, transfer to a serving bowl. Drizzle over a little of the warm vinaigrette to serve.

vegetarian

Gratin of roasted peppers, basil & feta

Serves 4

2 x 1lb (450g) jars ready-roasted peppers
   (ideally, mixed red and yellow peppers)
large bunch of basil
2 x 7oz (200g) packs feta cheese
black pepper
olive oil, to drizzle
Parmesan, for grating

Heat the oven to 425°F (220°C). Drain the peppers and slice in half if they are whole.

Arrange a layer of peppers in four small individual gratin dishes. Top with a handful of basil leaves, then crumble over a layer of feta. Season with pepper and drizzle with olive oil. Repeat these layers to reach the top of the dishes.

Grate some Parmesan over the top and grind over a little more pepper. Bake for 8 to 10 minutes or until the cheese is golden brown on top.

Quick minestrone

Serves 4

3–4 tbsp (45–60ml) olive oil
1 onion, peeled and diced
1 potato, peeled and diced
1 medium carrot, peeled and diced
1 kohlrabi, peeled and diced
2 bay leaves
few thyme sprigs
3oz (90g) dried spaghetti, broken into
 pieces
¼ savoy cabbage, cored and chopped
sea salt and black pepper
handful of Italian parsley, chopped
3oz (90g) Parmesan, freshly grated

Heat the olive oil in a large pan and add the onion, potato, carrot, kohlrabi, and herbs. Cook, stirring frequently, over high heat for 8 to 10 minutes until the vegetables are soft. Meanwhile, put the kettle on to boil.

Pour enough hot water over the vegetables to cover them and bring back to a boil. Add the spaghetti to the soup along with the cabbage and simmer for another 8 minutes or until the spaghetti is al dente.

Season the soup liberally and sprinkle generously with chopped parsley and grated Parmesan just before serving.

Nutty bulgur wheat with herbs

Serves 4

2¼ cups (300ml) bulgur wheat
½ cup (125ml) shelled pistachios, toasted
large handful of mixed herbs (eg Italian
 parsley, chervil, mint, and basil)
1½ tbsp (22ml) pomegranate molasses
1½ tbsp (22ml) lemon juice
6 tbsp (90ml) extra virgin olive oil, plus
 extra to drizzle (optional)
sea salt and black pepper

Put the bulgur wheat into a pan and pour over boiling water (from the kettle) to cover. Simmer for 10 to 12 minutes or until the grains are just tender. Meanwhile, coarsely chop the pistachios and herbs.

For the dressing, mix the pomegranate molasses, lemon juice, and olive oil together in a bowl. Season with salt and pepper to taste.

Drain the bulgur wheat thoroughly when it's ready, then immediately toss with the dressing, pistachios, and herbs. Taste and adjust the seasoning, and drizzle with a little more oil, if you wish. Serve warm or as a cold salad.

Easy vegetable curry

Serves 4

2 tbsp (30ml) vegetable oil

1 banana shallot (or 2 regular ones),
   peeled and roughly chopped

1 garlic clove, peeled and minced

2 long red chiles, seeded and minced

1 small celery root, peeled and chopped

sea salt and black pepper

3 tbsp (45ml) Madras curry paste

few cardamom pods

1 green bell pepper, cored, seeded, and
   roughly chopped

½ large cauliflower, cut into florets

14oz (398g) can chopped tomatoes

½ head of broccoli, cut into florets

1 large zucchini, roughly chopped

generous 1 cup (250ml) strained plain
   yogurt

Heat the oil in a large, wide pan and add the shallot, garlic, and chiles. Cook, stirring, for a minute or so until the garlic is fragrant.

Add the celery root and some seasoning. Cook over high heat for 2 minutes, then add the curry paste, cardamom pods, green bell pepper, and cauliflower florets. Continue to stir over high heat for a few more minutes.

Tip in the tomatoes, then fill the empty can with water and pour this in too. Bring to a boil, then add the broccoli and zucchini. Simmer for 8 to 10 minutes until the vegetables are tender.

Turn down the heat and stir in the yogurt. Taste and adjust the seasoning before serving.

Ratatouille

Serves 4

1 large red onion, peeled
1 small eggplant
1 red bell pepper, halved, cored, and
  seeded
1 yellow bell pepper, halved, cored, and
  seeded
1 large zucchini
4 tbsp (60ml) olive oil
few thyme sprigs
sea salt and black pepper
1 fat garlic clove, peeled and smashed
14oz (398g) can chopped tomatoes
8oz (225g) vine-ripened cherry tomatoes
small handful of basil leaves, roughly torn

Chop the vegetables
into bite-size pieces, keeping them separate. Heat the olive oil in a large pan and sauté the onion with the thyme sprigs and a little seasoning over high heat for a minute or two.

Add the eggplant,
red and yellow bell peppers, and the garlic. Sauté for a minute, then add the zucchini and sauté for another 2 minutes or so.

Tip in the canned tomatoes
and add a splash of water. Now add the cherry tomatoes and bring to a simmer. Cook for 8 to 10 minutes until the vegetables are just tender.

Season the ratatouille
with salt and pepper to taste, and sprinkle with basil before serving.

Cheap & cheerful
{everyday menu}

This easy menu is designed with a young family in mind. I don't know any child (or adult) who doesn't like chicken and flavorful mash. But the trick is always with the dessert. Promise your kids a banana split they cannot resist if they eat up their main course—it works like a charm with my lot. Serves 4.

Sticky lemon chicken
+ Champ   + green beans or sugar snap peas
Caramelized banana split

- Caramelize the bananas and make the chocolate sauce.
- Put the potatoes on to boil for the champ.
- Brown the chicken pieces, add the sauce ingredients, and let reduce.
- Drain the potatoes, make the champ, and keep warm.
- Serve the sticky lemon chicken and champ when ready.
- Assemble the caramelized banana splits just before serving.

STICKY LEMON CHICKEN

" If you have a jar of preserved lemons in the cupboard, chop up a lemon and add it to the sauce with a little more honey before reducing. It will give the dish a different dimension. **"**

Serves 4
1 large chicken, cut into 8–10 pieces
sea salt and black pepper
3–4 tbsp (45–60ml) olive oil
1 head of garlic, halved horizontally
few thyme sprigs
splash of sherry vinegar
2 tbsp (30ml) dark soy sauce
3 tbsp (45ml) honey
1 lemon, finely sliced (ideally with a
   mandolin)
bunch of Italian parsley, chopped

Season the chicken with salt and pepper and heat the olive oil in a large sauté pan. Brown the chicken pieces (in batches if necessary) over high heat with the garlic and thyme for 2 to 3 minutes on each side until golden brown. Return all the chicken to the pan, add the sherry vinegar, and bubble until reduced by half. Drizzle over the soy sauce and honey and shake the pan to mix.

Pour in a good splash of hot water and add the lemon slices. Let the liquid bubble and reduce down until syrupy, which will take about 10 minutes or so. By now the chicken should be cooked through.

Transfer the chicken to a platter and sprinkle over the chopped parsley. Serve with the champ and green beans or steamed sugar snap peas.

Champ

Cut the potatoes into similar-size chunks and boil in salted water for about 10 minutes until tender when pierced with a small sharp knife. Drain well.

Mash the potatoes while still hot, using a potato ricer if you have one, then stir through the butter and chopped green onions.

Pour the cream and milk into a pan and bring just to a boil. Take off the heat and gradually pour onto the potatoes, mixing well. If the mash is too thick, add a little extra milk. Season generously and serve.

Serves 4

2¼lb (1kg) mealy potatoes (eg round red), peeled

sea salt and black pepper

2 tbsp (30ml) butter

bunch of green onions (about 6–8), trimmed and chopped

⅓ cup (75ml) whipping cream

⅓ cup (75ml) whole milk, plus extra if needed

CARAMELIZED BANANA SPLIT

❝ Make sure you use good quality ice cream here. For extra child appeal, provide bowls with little extras, such as chocolate sprinkles and chocolate chips, so the kids can help themselves. ❞

Serves 4

4 ripe bananas

½ cup (125ml) superfine sugar

2–3 scoops each of different ice creams (eg vanilla, chocolate, strawberry)

⅔ cup (150ml) whipping cream, lightly whipped

shredded sweetened coconut, to sprinkle (optional)

4 candied (or pitted fresh) cherries

CHOCOLATE SAUCE:

4oz (125g) semisweet chocolate, broken into pieces

2 tbsp (30ml) runny honey

⅓ cup (75ml) whipping cream

Peel the bananas and cut in half lengthwise.
Place cut side up on a sturdy baking sheet and sprinkle evenly with the sugar. If you have a cook's blowtorch, wave it over the bananas until the sugar has caramelized. (Otherwise, preheat the broiler to its highest setting and flash the bananas under the broiler until golden brown and bubbling.) Let cool until the sugar has firmed up.

Make the chocolate sauce in the
meantime. Put all the ingredients in a bowl set over a pan of simmering water and stir occasionally until the chocolate has melted and the sauce is smooth. Take the bowl off the pan and let cool.

Arrange two banana halves on
clear serving dishes (ideally oval or oblong), with the caramelized sides facing outward. Place a scoop of each flavored ice cream between the banana halves. Drizzle with chocolate sauce, then spoon or pipe over the whipped cream. Sprinkle with the coconut if using and top each banana split with a cherry. Serve immediately.

fast fish 5

Tandoori spiced halibut with cucumber
Porgy with sweet onions & kale
Lemon sole with caper mayonnaise
Sea trout with fennel & watercress
Turbot with creamed cabbage & bacon

Tandoori spiced halibut with cucumber

Serves 4

4 skinned halibut fillets, about 5oz (150g) each

1 tbsp (15ml) tandoori or hot Madras curry paste

1 tbsp (15ml) olive oil

1 tsp (5ml) superfine sugar

2/3 cup (150ml) plain yogurt

2 cucumbers, peeled

handful of mint leaves, chopped

squeeze of lime juice

1–2 tbsp (15–30ml) vegetable oil

Heat the oven to 400°F (200°C). Lay the fish fillets on a plate. Mix the curry paste with the olive oil and sugar. Stir in all but 3 tbsp (45ml) of the yogurt. Coat the fish with the spiced yogurt and set aside.

Cut the cucumbers lengthwise, using a swivel vegetable peeler, into long wide strips, avoiding the seeds in the middle. Toss with the reserved yogurt, chopped mint, and lime juice.

Heat an ovenproof pan and add the vegetable oil. Scrape off the excess marinade from the halibut fillets and place them in the hot pan, reserving the marinade. Sear for 1 to 1½ minutes on each side until golden brown.

Spoon the marinade over the fish and place the pan in the oven for a few minutes to finish cooking. Transfer to warm plates, drizzle over the pan juices, and serve with the cucumber salad.

Porgy with sweet onions & kale

Serves 4

14oz (400g) kale, stalks removed, roughly
  shredded
sea salt and black pepper
4 tbsp (60ml) olive oil
2 large onions, peeled and sliced
2 tsp (10ml) superfine sugar
piece of butter
2 tbsp (30ml) sherry vinegar
4 porgy fillets, about 6oz (175g) each,
  skinned
¼ cup (50ml) fish or chicken stock

Add the kale to a pan of boiling salted water and blanch for 3 to 4 minutes. Drain in a colander, refresh under cold running water, and set aside.

Heat a sauté pan and add half the olive oil. Toss in the onions, season, and sprinkle with the sugar. Add a splash of water and cook over medium-high heat, stirring from time to time, for about 8 minutes until the onions are caramelized.

Add the blanched kale and a piece of butter. Toss well over the heat, then pour in the sherry vinegar and let bubble until it has reduced away.

Heat a large skillet with the remaining oil. Season the fish fillets and pan-fry for 2 to 2½ minutes until the fish is cooked two-thirds of the way through. Turn over and add the stock. Cook for 30 to 40 seconds until the fish is just cooked.

Divide the onions and kale among four serving plates. Place the fish fillets on top and pour over the juices from the pan. Serve immediately.

Lemon sole with caper mayonnaise

Serves 4

4 small (or 2 large) lemon sole, scaled
   and cleaned
olive oil, to drizzle
sea salt and black pepper
few thyme sprigs
1 lemon, quartered

CAPER MAYONNAISE:
generous ¾ cup (175ml) mayonnaise
   (see page 248)
1 gherkin, minced
1 tbsp (15ml) capers, drained and chopped
1 tbsp (15ml) chopped Italian parsley
½ small garlic clove, peeled and crushed
squeeze of lemon juice

Heat the oven to 400°F (200°C). Score the lemon sole at intervals along their length. Lightly oil two large baking sheets and sprinkle with salt and pepper. Scatter over a few sprigs of thyme.

Lay the fish on top and drizzle with more olive oil. Sprinkle the fish with salt, pepper, and some thyme leaves. Roast for about 15 to 20 minutes, depending on the size of the fish. It is cooked when the thickest part of the flesh pulls away easily from the bone.

Mix the ingredients for the caper mayonnaise together in the meantime. Season with salt and pepper to taste and add a little more lemon juice or water if you prefer a thinner consistency.

Serve the sole whole (or filleted if you've cooked 2 large fish) with the caper mayonnaise and lemon wedges for squeezing over.

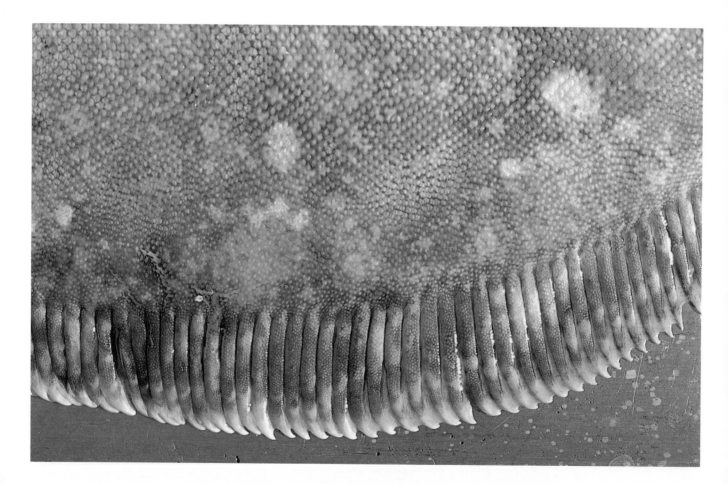

Sea trout with fennel & watercress

Serves 4

4 fennel bulbs, trimmed and tough outer leaves removed
1 tsp (5ml) fennel seeds
sea salt and black pepper
5 tbsp (75ml) olive oil, plus extra to drizzle
1½ tsp (7ml) superfine sugar
1 tbsp (15ml) sherry vinegar
4 sea trout fillets, with skin, about 5oz (150g) each
bunch of watercress, about 4oz (125g), well washed and stems removed

Slice the fennel bulbs thinly. Crush the fennel seeds with a little salt using a mortar and pestle. Heat 3 tbsp (45ml) olive oil in a pan and add the sliced fennel and crushed fennel seeds. Sprinkle over the sugar and cook over high heat for 10 minutes, stirring well. Add the sherry vinegar and cook for another 5 minutes until the fennel is soft and caramelized.

Score the skin of the sea trout fillets at close intervals with a sharp knife. Heat the remaining oil in a wide sauté pan. Season the fish and cook, skin side down, until cooked two-thirds of the way through. Flip over and cook on the other side for 30 seconds.

Divide the fennel among four plates and sit the fish fillets on top. Garnish with watercress, drizzle with olive oil, and serve.

Turbot with creamed cabbage & bacon

Serves 4

4 tbsp (60ml) olive oil

6 slices of unsmoked lean bacon, derinded and chopped

1 large carrot, peeled and diced

½ celery root, peeled and diced

½ savoy cabbage, cored and finely shredded

¾ cup (175ml) whipping cream

sea salt and black pepper

4 turbot fillets, about 5oz (150g) each, skinned

large piece of butter

juice of ½ lemon

large handful of Italian parsley, chopped

Heat half of the olive oil in a large pan. Add the chopped bacon and cook for a few minutes, then stir in the carrot and celery root. Cover the pan with a tight-fitting lid and cook for 8 to 10 minutes over medium heat until the celery root turns translucent.

Add the shredded cabbage and cook for 3 to 4 minutes, then pour in the cream. Simmer for a few minutes until the cream has thickened and the cabbage is tender. Season well and keep warm.

Meanwhile, heat a sauté pan and add the remaining olive oil. Season the fish with salt and pepper. When the pan is hot, add the fish, skinned side down, and pan-fry for 1½ minutes until golden brown on the underside.

Flip the fish over and add the butter to the pan. Squeeze over the lemon juice and let bubble gently for 1 to 2 minutes. Toss in the parsley and spoon the herby butter over the fish. Take off the heat.

Spoon the creamed cabbage into the middle of four warm plates and top with the turbot fillets. Spoon any remaining pan juices over the fish and serve.

174

Summer special

{entertaining menu}

I love the simplicity of this menu. Full of summery flavors, it kicks off with a refreshing chilled soup, followed by tasty baked salmon fillets and a colorful tomato salad. Serve a cold glass of Vin Santo with the roasted nectarines for a perfect finish. Serves 4.

Avocado & cucumber soup
Salmon with Mediterranean flavors
        + Mixed tomato salad
Roasted nectarines with amaretti cream

- Make the soup and chill.
- Preheat the oven and stud the salmon with the flavorings.
- Prepare the tomato salad and dressing.
- Halve and pit the nectarines. Crush the amaretti.
- Put the salmon in the oven to bake.
- Prepare the amaretti cream and chill.
- When the salmon is ready, rest in a warm place while you serve the soup.
- Bake the nectarines.
- Dress the tomato salad and serve with the salmon.
- Plate the nectarines and amaretti cream to serve.

AVOCADO & CUCUMBER SOUP

" Use really ripe avocados to give this soup a rich green color. If you want to take it a step further, add some cooked lobster or flaky crabmeat, or perhaps one or two Norway lobsters (Dublin Bay prawns), to the garnish. The perfect cooling appetizer, this soup can also be served as a light summer lunch with a crusty baguette. **"**

Serves 4
2 large cucumbers, about 14oz (400g) each, chilled
juice of 1 lemon, or to taste
2 ripe avocados
2 tbsp (30ml) strained plain yogurt
1 tbsp (15ml) Worcestershire sauce
sea salt and black pepper
½ red onion, minced
1 plum tomato, seeded and minced
1 tbsp (15ml) olive oil, plus extra to drizzle
3–4 basil leaves, finely shredded

Peel the cucumbers, quarter lengthwise, and remove the seeds. Dice a quarter and set aside for the garnish. Roughly chop the rest, place in a blender with half the lemon juice, and whiz until smooth.

Halve, pit, and peel the avocados. Mince one avocado half to use for the garnish. Squeeze over a little lemon juice and set aside with the diced cucumber. Tip the rest of the avocados into the blender.

Blend the avocados with the puréed cucumber, strained plain yogurt, and Worcestershire sauce until very smooth. Season generously with salt and pepper, and add lemon juice to taste. Chill until ready to serve.

For the garnish, combine the diced cucumber and avocado with the red onion and tomato. Toss with the olive oil and shredded basil.

Taste the chilled soup for seasoning and add a splash of cold water if it is too thick. Pour into four chilled bowls and spoon the garnish into the center. Add a drizzle of olive oil and grind over a little pepper to serve.

SALMON WITH MEDITERRANEAN FLAVORS

"Studding salmon fillets with sun-dried tomato, basil, olive, and garlic imparts some strong flavors and gives the fish a different character."

Serves 4

4 skinned salmon fillets, about 7oz (200g) each

¼ cup (50ml) sun-dried tomatoes in oil, halved if large

handful of basil leaves

¼ cup (50ml) pitted black olives

3 large garlic cloves, peeled and thinly sliced

sea salt and black pepper

olive oil, to drizzle

Heat the oven to 400°F (200°C). Place the salmon fillets on a board, skinned side down. Use an apple corer to make 6 small holes in each fillet.

Flatten the sun-dried tomatoes and place a basil leaf, an olive, and a sliver of garlic on each one. Roll up and use to stuff the holes in the salmon. Season with salt and pepper.

Place the salmon fillets on a lightly oiled baking sheet. Drizzle with olive oil and bake for 6 to 8 minutes until medium-rare—the thickest part will feel slightly springy when pressed. Place on warm plates and serve with the tomato salad and country bread.

Mixed tomato salad

Halve larger tomatoes or cut into quarters; keep smaller ones whole. Place in a large serving bowl.

For the dressing, whisk the mustard, wine vinegar, sugar, and olive oil together and season with salt and pepper to taste. (Or shake to combine in a screw-topped jar.)

Drizzle the dressing over the tomatoes and toss gently. Scatter the torn basil over the salad to serve.

Serves 4

1⅓lb (600g) mixed vine-ripened tomatoes (eg red and yellow cherry, plum, romano, green zebra)

handful of basil leaves, torn

DRESSING:

1 tsp (5ml) Dijon mustard

1 tbsp (15ml) red wine vinegar

½ tsp (2ml) superfine sugar

4 tbsp (60ml) extra virgin olive oil

sea salt and black pepper

ROASTED NECTARINES
WITH AMARETTI CREAM

66 This works equally well with peaches—just make sure you use ripe, firm, juicy fruit. Immature nectarines or peaches would simply disappoint. **99**

Serves 4
4 ripe nectarines
a little oil, to oil
3–4 tbsp (45–60ml) confectioners' sugar
few pieces of butter
⅔ cup (150ml) whipping cream
generous 1 cup (250g) mascarpone
1 tbsp (15ml) amaretto liqueur (or milk)
2oz (50g) amaretti cookies, lightly crushed

Heat the oven to 400°F (200°C). Halve the nectarines, prise out the pits, then place cut side up on a lightly oiled baking sheet.

Dust the nectarines with the confectioners' sugar and top each one with a piece of butter. Bake for 10 to 12 minutes or until the sugar topping has slightly caramelized. Place two nectarine halves on each shallow serving bowl and let cool slightly.

For the amaretti cream, whip the cream until soft peaks form. In another bowl, stir the mascarpone with the amaretto (or milk) to lighten it, then fold through the softly whipped cream. Fold through two-thirds of the crushed cookies.

Top the baked nectarines with the amaretti cream and sprinkle over the remaining crushed cookies. Serve at once.

Fast ways to cook meat

Buy tender cuts, apply suitable cooking techniques, and tasty meat dishes can be on the table in no time:

Stir-frying Invest in a large, traditional wok (unless you already have one). Use tender cuts, like chicken breasts, beef tenderloin, pork tenderloin, and lamb fillet. Cut the meat (and flavoring vegetables) into small strips to ensure fast, even cooking and have everything ready before you start. Heat the wok over high heat, add the oil, then get stir-frying.

Fast roasting Tender joints of meat such as rack of lamb, pork tenderloin, and beef tenderloin can be roasted at a high temperature and take little time to cook. The meat should be trimmed or shaped to an even thickness to ensure even cooking and it must be rested after roasting—for at least 15 minutes.

Grilling and broiling Using intense heat, these methods produce succulent meat—brown and crisp on the outside and juicy within. Buy tender cuts—no thicker then 2 inches (5cm), otherwise the meat will be charred on the outside before it is cooked in the center. Preheat the broiler or grill to high and don't leave the meat unattended while it's cooking.

Pan-frying Chops, steaks, and chicken breasts lend themselves to pan-frying in a little olive oil and/or butter. You'll need a large, wide heavy skillet—avoid overcrowding, otherwise the meat will stew rather than fry. Get the skillet hot before you add the meat, but be ready to adjust the heat during cooking. Again, let the meat rest after cooking and do deglaze the pan with a little wine, stock, or other liquor to retain all the tasty caramelized meat juices.

5

meat

Quail with kohlrabi & butternut squash
Loin chops with garlic & herb butter
Beef rib-eye with baby turnips in port
Veal scallop with sautéed vegetables
Venison with sweet & sour peppers

Quail with kohlrabi & butternut squash

Serves 4

8 oven-ready quails, legs removed
    (leaving the crown and wing tips)
sea salt and black pepper
2 tbsp (30ml) olive oil, plus extra
    to drizzle
2 tbsp (30ml) butter, cut into cubes
few thyme sprigs
1 butternut squash, 1½–1¾lb (700–800g),
    peeled, seeded, and cut into ¾-inch
    (2cm) cubes
1 kohlrabi, about 14oz (400g), peeled and
    cut into ¾-inch (2cm) cubes

Heat the oven to 400°F (200°C) and put a large roasting pan inside to heat up.

Season the quails and sear in a hot heavy pan with the olive oil over high heat until golden brown all over (you may need to do this in two batches). Add the butter and thyme, spooning the butter into the quail cavities as it melts. Transfer the birds to a plate.

Toss the squash and kohlrabi into the pan. Season well and cook over high heat for 2 to 3 minutes. Tip them into the hot roasting pan and sit the quails on top. Cook in the oven for 10 minutes. Lift the quails onto a warm platter and rest for 5 minutes. Return the vegetables to the oven for another 5 minutes or until they are tender.

To serve, divide the roasted vegetables among warm plates and place 2 quails on top. Drizzle with a little olive oil and serve.

Loin chops with garlic & herb butter

Serves 4

3 tbsp (45ml) olive oil
4 double loin chops, about 12oz (350g)
  each and 1½ inches (4cm) thick
few thyme sprigs

GARLIC AND HERB BUTTER:
4 tbsp (60ml) unsalted butter, softened
1 fat garlic clove, peeled and finely
  crushed
handful of Italian parsley, chopped
small handful of mint, chopped
sea salt and black pepper

For the garlic and herb butter, blend the softened butter with the garlic, chopped herbs, and some seasoning. Spoon onto a piece of plastic wrap and shape into a neat roll, wrapping the butter in the plastic wrap and twisting the ends to seal. Pop into the freezer to chill while you prepare the chops (or in the refrigerator for at least 30 minutes if preparing ahead).

Heat the olive oil in a large skillet. (You may need to use two pans.) Season the chops with salt and pepper, then lift into the pan and add the thyme sprigs. Pan-fry for 2½ to 3 minutes on each side, spooning the pan juices over the chops as they cook. The chops are ready when the meat feels slightly springy if lightly pressed.

Transfer the chops to a warm platter and rest for a few minutes. Unwrap the garlic and herb butter and cut into 4 thick slices. Place a slice on top of each chop. The warmth of the chops will soon melt the butter, so serve them quickly.

Beef rib-eye with baby turnips in port

Serves 4

5 tbsp (75ml) olive oil
14oz (400g) baby turnips, washed
few thyme sprigs
sea salt and black pepper
1 tsp (5ml) Chinese five-spice powder
few pieces of butter
¾ cup (175ml) port
1 tsp (5ml) soft brown sugar
4 boneless rib-eye of beef steaks, about
  9oz (250g) each and 1¼ inches (3cm)
  thick, trimmed

Heat half the olive oil in a heavy pan and add the turnips, thyme, and seasoning. Sauté for a minute, then add the five-spice and a couple of pieces of butter. Cook, tossing occasionally, for 8 to 10 minutes until golden brown.

Pour in the port, standing well back as it may flambé. Sprinkle in the sugar, stirring to dissolve, then let bubble for about 5 minutes until the liquor is reduced and syrupy.

Season the beef and sear in a hot ovenproof pan with the remaining oil. Pan-fry for 3 to 4 minutes on each side, adding a piece of butter to finish off the cooking. For medium-rare beef, the meat should be slightly springy when pressed. Rest the steaks in a warm place for 5 minutes before serving, with the glazed turnips.

Veal scallop with sautéed vegetables

Serves 4

**4 veal scallops, about 6oz (175g)
each and ¼ inch (5mm) thick
4 tbsp (60ml) all-purpose flour
3 tbsp (45ml) olive oil**

**SAUTÉED VEGETABLES:
1 red bell pepper, cored and seeded
1 yellow bell pepper, cored and seeded
1 medium eggplant, trimmed
1 zucchini, trimmed
4 tbsp (60ml) olive oil
1 garlic clove (unpeeled), smashed
few thyme sprigs
sea salt and black pepper
splash of balsamic vinegar**

Mince the vegetables. Heat 3 tbsp (45ml) olive oil in a large skillet with the garlic. Tip in the bell peppers, eggplant, and thyme, and cook over high heat for 3 to 4 minutes. Add the zucchini.

Season and sauté for 2 minutes until the vegetables are just tender. Take off the heat and dress with the remaining olive oil and balsamic vinegar; check the seasoning. Keep warm.

Coat the veal all over with the flour seasoned with salt and pepper, shaking off any excess. Heat the olive oil in a wide pan and sauté the veal over high heat for 1½ minutes on each side until golden brown. (Do this in two batches if your pan is not wide enough.)

Transfer the scallops to warm plates and spoon the sautéed vegetables over them to serve.

Venison with sweet & sour peppers

Serves 4

4 venison loin steaks, about 6oz (175g)
  each and 1¼ inches (3cm) thick
6–7 tbsp (90–105ml) olive oil, plus extra
  to drizzle
sea salt and black pepper
1 tbsp (15ml) juniper berries, lightly
  crushed
handful of thyme sprigs
3 red bell peppers, cored, seeded, and
  sliced
3 yellow bell peppers, cored, seeded,
  and sliced
2 tbsp (30ml) white wine vinegar

TIP If you've had time to plan
ahead, marinate the venison with the olive
oil, juniper berries, and thyme overnight to
help tenderize the meat.

Place the venison in a shallow dish and drizzle with
2–3 tbsp (30–45ml) olive oil. Season lightly with salt and pepper and
scatter over the juniper berries and a few thyme sprigs. Let marinate
while you cook the bell peppers.

Heat 2 tbsp (30ml) olive oil in a large pan and add the red
and yellow bell peppers with a little seasoning. Add a few thyme sprigs
and cook over medium heat for about 5 minutes. Pour in the wine
vinegar and let bubble until the liquid has reduced right down. Remove
from the heat and keep warm.

Season the venison with salt and pepper. Heat
another heavy pan, then add the remaining olive oil. When it is very
hot, sear the venison fillets for 3 to 4 minutes on each side. Let rest in a
warm place for 5 minutes.

Divide the peppers among warm plates. Slice the
venison fillets thickly on the diagonal and arrange on top of the
peppers. Drizzle with a little olive oil to serve.

Indian spice
{everyday menu}

Based on the fragrant spices of southern Indian cooking, this pilau has a wonderful flavor, without the sweat-inducing kick of a fiery curry. Of course, you can spice it up with a few chopped chiles if you like. Minty grilled pineapple is a refreshing finish. Serves 4.

Shrimp pilau
Wilted spinach with mustard seeds
Grilled pineapple with mint & toasted coconut

- Preheat the oven.
- Make the mint syrup and grill the pineapple for the dessert; cool.
- Prepare the shrimp pilau and put in the oven to cook.
- Skin and slice the pineapple, toss with the mint syrup, and chill.
- Wash and drain the spinach; prepare the flavoring ingredients.
- Remove the pilau from the oven and let stand for 5 minutes.
- Sauté the spinach.
- Serve the main course.
- Scatter mint and toasted coconut over the pineapple and serve.

SHRIMP PILAU

> This mildly spiced Indian pilau is a terrific, easy one-pot supper. You can keep it simple and just use jumbo shrimp as suggested, or add other seafood such as sliced baby squid and/or firm fish like hake or halibut.

Serves 4

2 cups (500ml) light chicken stock
4 tbsp (60ml) olive oil
1 large onion, peeled and minced
1 garlic clove, peeled and chopped
1 tsp (5ml) ground cumin
1 tsp (5ml) ground coriander
1½ tsp (7ml) mild curry powder
10 cardamom pods
few thyme sprigs (leaves only)
7oz (200g) basmati rice
sea salt and black pepper
20 large jumbo shrimp (in shells)

Heat the oven to 400°F (200°C). Cut a circle of baking parchment, big enough to generously cover a wide ovenproof pan. Cut a steam hole in the center (fold the paper into segments, snip off the tip, then open.) Bring the stock to a boil in another pan.

Heat the olive oil in the ovenproof pan and add the onion, garlic, spices, and thyme. Stir over medium heat for 2 to 3 minutes, then tip in the rice and stir well. Add some salt and pepper and toast the rice for a minute. Pour in the boiling stock and quickly arrange the shrimp on top of the rice in a single layer.

Lay the parchment on top to cover, then transfer the pan to the oven. Bake for 10 to 12 minutes or until the rice is just tender and has absorbed most of the liquid. Let stand, still covered with the paper, for 5 minutes before serving.

Wilted spinach with mustard seeds

Heat the oil in a large pan and cook the onion, garlic, and ginger for 3 to 4 minutes until the onion begins to soften. Stir in the garam masala and mustard seeds and toast the spices for a minute until fragrant. (The mustard seeds may pop and jump out of the pan when heated; if so, cover with a lid for a few seconds.)

Throw in the spinach leaves a large handful at a time and stir quickly until the leaves begin to wilt. Season with salt and pepper to taste and serve.

Serves 4

3 tbsp (45ml) vegetable oil
1 large onion, peeled and finely sliced
1 garlic clove, peeled and finely grated
¾-inch (2cm) piece of fresh ginger, peeled and finely grated
½ tsp (2ml) garam masala
1 tsp (5ml) brown or black mustard seeds
14oz (400g) spinach leaves, washed
sea salt and black pepper

197

GRILLED PINEAPPLE
WITH MINT & TOASTED COCONUT

❝ Grilling pineapple helps to draw out its natural sweetness, which is particularly useful if you find the fruit is slightly underripe when you cut into it. If you're thinking ahead, prepare this dessert the night before—to give the pineapple plenty of time to infuse with the mint syrup. ❞

Serves 4
generous ⅓ cup (75ml) superfine
  sugar
small bunch of mint, plus shredded
  mint leaves to finish
1 large ripe pineapple
scant ¼ cup (50ml) dry unsweetened
  coconut, toasted

Put the sugar in a pan, add ⅔ cup (150ml) water and stir over low heat until the sugar has dissolved. Increase the heat and bring to a boil. Throw in the mint sprigs, turn off the heat, and let infuse the syrup as it cools.

Cut the pineapple into 8 wedges and cut out the core. Heat a grill (or barbecue). Add the pineapple and grill for 2 to 3 minutes on each side until charred. Let cool slightly.

Cut away the skin from the pineapple, then slice the grilled flesh thinly and place in a bowl. Take out the mint sprigs, then pour the infused syrup over the pineapple wedges. Chill until ready to serve.

Divide the pineapple among individual bowls and spoon over the syrup. Sprinkle with the shredded mint leaves and toasted coconut to serve.

fast 5 side dishes

Couscous, fava beans, peas & pancetta
Mixed vegetable stir-fry
Crunchy broccoli & cauliflower gratin
Sautéed potatoes with panch phora
Spicy fried rice with green onions

Couscous, fava beans, peas & pancetta

Serves 4

Pan-fry 9oz (250g) chopped pancetta in a little olive oil until crisp. Remove with a slotted spoon and drain; save the oil in the pan.

Tip 1¼ cups (300ml) couscous into a bowl and pour on 1¾ cups (425ml) hot chicken or vegetable stock. Add a squeeze of lemon juice and the reserved oil. Give the mixture a stir and cover the bowl with plastic wrap. Let stand for 5 to 8 minutes.

Meanwhile, blanch 5oz (150g) fresh fava beans and 5oz (150g) peas in boiling water for 2 minutes. Refresh and drain well.

Fluff up the couscous with a fork. Add the pancetta, beans, peas, and a handful of chopped mint and Italian parsley. Season and drizzle generously with olive oil. Fork through and serve.

Mixed vegetable stir-fry

Serves 4

Slice 2 carrots, 2 celery stalks, and ½ each sliced red, yellow, and green bell pepper, keeping them separate.

Heat a wok until very hot, then add 2 tbsp (30ml) each vegetable and sesame oil. Add 1 chopped garlic clove and the sliced carrots and stir-fry for 30 seconds.

Toss in the sliced bell peppers and stir-fry for another 30 seconds, then add the sliced celery and 7oz (200g) bean sprouts and toss over the heat for another 30 seconds.

Add 1 tbsp (15ml) dark soy sauce and 3 tbsp (45ml) oyster sauce and mix well. Scatter with toasted sesame seeds and serve.

Crunchy broccoli & cauliflower gratin

Serves 4

Heat the oven to 400°F (200°C). Cut a small cauliflower and a head of broccoli into florets. Add the cauliflower to a large pan of boiling salted water and blanch for 1 minute. Tip in the broccoli and cook for another 2 minutes. Drain well and tip into a bowl.

Beat generous ¾ cup (175ml) crème fraîche with 2 large egg yolks and some salt and pepper. Pour over the vegetables and toss well, then tip into an oiled large gratin dish.

Scatter over ½ cup (125ml) lightly crushed toasted hazelnuts and top with a generous grating of Parmesan. Bake for 10 minutes or until the topping is golden brown. For a crisp topping, flash under a hot broiler for a few minutes before serving.

Sautéed potatoes with panch phora

Serves 4

Peel 6 medium potatoes (eg round red) and cut into ½-inch (1cm) thick slices. Add to a pan of boiling salted water and boil for 6 minutes until just tender. Drain well and pat dry between sheets of paper towels.

Heat 2 tbsp (30ml) olive oil in a large sauté pan over high heat. Add the potato slices and season with salt and pepper. Pan-fry for about 3 minutes on each side until lightly golden.

Sprinkle with 1 tbsp (15ml) panch phora spice mix and add a piece of butter to the pan. Sauté for 1 to 2 minutes, tossing and turning the potatoes in the spices, until golden brown and crisp at the edges. Serve immediately.

TIP Panch phora is a blend of five spices: brown mustard seeds, nigella seeds, fenugreek, cumin, and fennel. If you can't find it, use ½ tsp (2ml) of each spice for this dish.

Spicy fried rice with green onions

Serves 4

TIP For an extra spicy and fiery kick, stir in 1 tsp (5ml) sambal oelek, a Southeast Asian spice paste, with the rice.

Heat a wok until very hot, then add 2 tbsp (30ml) vegetable oil and 1 tbsp (15ml) sesame oil. Throw in 1 tsp (5ml) freshly grated ginger and 1 chopped garlic clove, and stir-fry for a minute until fragrant.

Toss in 3 cups (750ml) cooked basmati (or jasmine) rice along with 5 or 6 chopped green onions. Add a generous splash of dark soy sauce and 2–3 tbsp (30–45ml) sweet chili sauce. Stir-fry for a couple of minutes until the rice is piping hot. Drizzle with a little more sesame oil to taste, then serve.

Thai feast
{entertaining menu}

I think of this as a celebration of Thai food—each dish highlighting the balance of sweet, sour, salty, and hot flavors that are typical of the cuisine. It's worth trying to get hold of the authentic ingredients, especially if you have access to a good Asian grocery store, though I have suggested alternatives for the more unusual ingredients. Serves 4.

planning your menu

Yam pak salad
Thai red lobster curry
+ steamed jasmine rice
+ Chinese greens with shiitake mushrooms
Lychees with mint sugar

- Make the dressing for the salad and let cool.
- Peel the lychees and chill. Make the mint sugar.
- Cook the rice and make the curry (but don't add the lobster yet).
- Prepare the salad ingredients, toss with the dressing, and serve.
- Add the lobster to the curry to warm through.
- Stir-fry the Chinese greens with shiitake mushrooms.
- Serve the lobster curry with rice and the Chinese greens.
- Serve the lychees with mint sugar.

YAM PAK SALAD

66 I adore the combination of flavors in this fruity salad, which is perfectly complemented by the tamarind dressing. If you can't find Asian pears, substitute crisp green or red apples. For an authentic finish and extra crunch, I finish with a sprinkling of crispy fried shallots, which you can buy in small tubs from Asian food stores. Use chopped, roasted peanuts, if you prefer. 99

Serves 4

1 large green or underripe mango

2 Asian pears

1 carambola, trimmed

1 banana shallot, peeled and sliced into rings

large bunch of sweet Thai basil (leaves only), shredded

large bunch of mint (leaves only), shredded

2–3 tbsp (30–45ml) crispy fried shallots (optional)

DRESSING:

1 tbsp (15ml) tamarind paste

2 tbsp (30ml) Thai fish sauce

2 tbsp (30ml) palm (or soft dark brown) sugar

2 tbsp (30ml) lime juice

2 tbsp (30ml) sesame oil

TIP If using packed tamarind with seeds, put 1oz (30g) in a small bowl and pour on a little boiling water. Stir to break it up into small pieces and let soak for 10 minutes. Push through a fine strainer to remove the seeds and use the strained juice.

First make the dressing. Put all the ingredients into a pan and stir over medium heat until the sugar has dissolved and the dressing is smooth. Take off the heat and let cool completely.

Peel the mango and thinly slice the flesh away from the seed. Quarter, core, and thinly slice the Asian pears. Thinly slice the carambola.

Place the fruit, shallot rings, and herbs in a large bowl, drizzle over the cooled dressing, and toss gently to mix.

Pile the salad onto individual plates and garnish with a sprinkling of crispy shallots if you like, to serve.

THAI RED LOBSTER CURRY

" Nothing beats a good Thai curry and this one is so easy. The lobster tastes divine, but you can use monkfish, or strips of chicken, lamb, or beef tenderloin— adding them at the start with the curry paste. If you can't get Japanese eggplants (available from Asian food stores), use a regular eggplant or white mushrooms. "

Serves 4
2 tbsp (30ml) vegetable oil
3 tbsp (45ml) red curry paste
1¾ cups (425ml) coconut milk
1 tbsp (15ml) Thai fish sauce
4–5 kaffir lime leaves
7oz (200g) Japanese eggplants, stalks removed
4 cooked lobster tails, shelled
7oz (200g) canned bamboo shoots
sea salt and black pepper
1 tsp (5ml) superfine sugar
squeeze of lime juice

Heat a large pan and add the oil, followed by the curry paste. Sauté over medium heat, stirring continuously, for 2 minutes until the paste is fragrant. Add the coconut milk, fish sauce, and lime leaves and bring to a boil.

Add the eggplants and cook for 5 minutes. Meanwhile, slice the lobster tails into large bite-size pieces.

Drain the bamboo shoots, add to the curry, and simmer for a couple of minutes. Tip in the lobster pieces and warm through briefly. Season with salt and pepper, and add the sugar and lime juice to taste. Serve at once, with rice.

Chinese greens with shiitake mushrooms

Trim the Chinese greens and broccoli and halve the stems if they are too long to fit in a wok.

Heat a large wok and add the oils. Tip in the shallot and mushrooms and stir-fry for 2 minutes. Add the garlic and stir-fry for another minute.

Toss in the greens and broccoli, then add the soy and oyster sauces with a splash of water. Bring to a boil and keep tossing and turning over the heat for a couple of minutes until the greens are just tender. Drizzle over a little more sesame oil and transfer to a warm platter to serve.

Serves 4
14oz (400g) Chinese greens (eg Chinese broccoli or bok choy)
7oz (200g) tender stem broccoli
2 tbsp (30ml) vegetable oil
1 tbsp (15ml) sesame oil, plus extra to drizzle
1 banana shallot, peeled and thinly sliced
7oz (200g) shiitake mushrooms, stalks removed and sliced
1 large garlic clove, peeled and thinly sliced
2 tbsp (30ml) dark soy sauce
3 tbsp (45ml) oyster sauce

LYCHEES WITH MINT SUGAR

" If you are short of time, simply put a large bowl of lychees on the table and provide each guest with a small dipping bowl of mint sugar. Everyone can help themselves and peel their own lychees at their leisure. **"**

Serves 4
1lb 2oz (500g) fresh lychees
¼ cup (50ml) granulated sugar
pinch of sea salt
small bunch of mint, leaves only

Peel the lychees and divide among individual serving bowls.

Put the sugar, salt, and mint leaves in a food processor and pulse for a few seconds only, until the mixture turns bright green. Do not overprocess or the mint will turn black.

Spoon the mint sugar into four small dipping bowls to serve with the lychees.

fruity desserts

5

Pain perdu with raspberries & ricotta
Creamy mango dessert
Cherries with almonds & mint
Figs & blackberries poached in red wine
Berry & Champagne soup

Pain perdu with raspberries & ricotta

Serves 4

½ cup (125ml) ricotta cheese, drained
½ cup (125ml) mascarpone
2 tbsp (30ml) superfine sugar
squeeze of lemon juice
7oz (200g) raspberries
2 tbsp (30ml) unsalted butter
4 slices raisin bread
3 large eggs, beaten
few basil sprigs, to finish
confectioners' sugar, to sprinkle

Beat the ricotta, mascarpone, sugar, and lemon juice together in a bowl, then gently fold through half of the raspberries to get a rippled effect.

Melt the butter in a wide, nonstick skillet until it begins to foam. Dip the raisin bread into the beaten eggs, add to the skillet, and pan-fry for a minute or two on each side until golden brown. Place each slice on a serving plate.

Spoon the ricotta mixture onto the warm pain perdu and tumble the remaining raspberries on top. Finish with basil sprigs and a sprinkling of confectioners' sugar to serve.

Creamy mango dessert

Serves 4

1 large ripe mango
1–2 tbsp (15–30ml) superfine sugar
 (optional)
1¼ cups (300ml) heavy cream

Peel the mango and carefully cut the flesh away from the seed. Cut a quarter into neat, thin slices and set aside. Chop the rest into rough chunks.

Whiz the chunks of mango to a smooth purée in a blender or food processor, adding sugar to taste. (You may not need any if the mango is perfectly ripe.)

Whip the cream until soft peaks form, then lightly fold in three-quarters of the mango purée.

Divide the cream mix among serving glasses and spoon the remaining mango purée on top. Decorate each serving with a few slices of mango.

Cherries with almonds & mint

Serves 4

1lb 2oz (500g) ripe cherries, pitted
1–2 tbsp (15–30ml) superfine sugar
splash of amaretto liqueur
squeeze of lemon juice
½ cup (125ml) slivered almonds, toasted
small handful of mint leaves, chopped
clotted cream (Devonshire cream) or
　crème fraîche, to serve

Warm the cherries and sugar in a nonstick pan until the sugar begins to dissolve and the cherries start to release their juices. Add the amaretto and lemon juice and cook for a few more minutes until the liquid has reduced down.

Divide the cherries among small serving bowls and scatter over the toasted almonds and chopped mint.

Serve topped with a generous dollop of clotted cream (Devonshire cream) or crème fraîche.

Figs & blackberries poached in red wine

Serves 4

1 vanilla bean

generous 1 cup (250ml) red wine (eg a
   young Merlot)

1 cinnamon stick

4 cloves

2 star anise

½ cup (125ml) sugar

3 figs, cut into quarters

1lb 2oz (500g) blackberries

generous 1 cup (250ml) mascarpone

2 tbsp (30ml) confectioners' sugar

Split the vanilla bean lengthwise, scrape out the
seeds with the back of the knife, and set aside.

Put the wine, empty vanilla bean, cinnamon stick, cloves,
star anise, and sugar into a pan and slowly bring to a boil, stirring to
dissolve the sugar. Lower the heat to a simmer, add the fruit, and
poach gently for 8 to 10 minutes. Let cool completely.

Put the mascarpone into a bowl and sift in the
confectioners' sugar. Add the reserved vanilla seeds and beat well.

Divide the poached fruit among four bowls
and serve with the vanilla mascarpone.

Berry & Champagne soup

Serves 4

4oz (125g) blackberries

4oz (125g) blueberries

4oz (125g) red currants

4oz (125g) raspberries

handful of mint leaves

2–3 tbsp (30–45ml) superfine sugar

¾ cup (175ml) plain yogurt

¾ cup (175ml) whipping cream

1¼ cups (300ml) Champagne or
   sparkling wine, chilled

TIP A great way to use up the last of the season's berries, particularly if you have some overripe fruit in the refrigerator. Freeze them before blending for a refreshing dessert.

Tip all the berries into a blender and whiz to a purée. Add the mint leaves and sugar to taste, and blitz until the mint is minced. Pour in the yogurt, cream, and Champagne and whiz until evenly blended and frothy.

Pour the soup into serving glasses or individual bowls and serve immediately.

Speedy sunday lunch
{everyday menu}

I love a traditional roast, but sometimes there just isn't enough time. When the first warm sunny days appear in spring, Tana and I want to be outdoors with the kids making the most of them. This is the perfect menu—quick, easy, and full of spring flavors—young tender lamb, fresh peas, and tart gooseberries. Serves 4.

planning your menu

New season's lamb with crushed peas
+ minted new potatoes
Crunchy gooseberry crumble

- Preheat the oven.
- Prepare the gooseberries and divide among baking dishes.
- Prepare the crumble topping.
- Poach the lamb.
- Boil the new potatoes and blanch the fresh peas.
- Set the lamb aside to rest for 10 minutes.
- Assemble the crumble and bake.
- Blend the peas and warm through.
- Drain the potatoes and toss in butter with some chopped mint.
- Slice the lamb, plate with the crushed peas, and serve with the potatoes.
- Remove crumble from oven and let stand for 5 to 10 minutes before serving.

NEW SEASON'S LAMB WITH CRUSHED PEAS

" People don't generally think of poaching lamb, but I find it's a really good way to cook this pink, delicate meat and ensure a succulent, flavorful result, particularly if you add lots of aromatics to the cooking liquor as I do. **"**

Serves 4

4 rumps of new season's lamb, about 4¾oz (140g) each, trimmed

3⅓ cups (825ml) chicken stock

few thyme sprigs

1 bay leaf

1 tbsp (15ml) black peppercorns

1 tbsp (15ml) coriander seeds

10oz (300g) fresh peas (or frozen and thawed)

generous drizzle of olive oil

2 tbsp (30ml) chopped oregano, plus extra leaves to garnish

sea salt and black pepper

extra virgin olive oil, to drizzle

Place the lamb rumps in a cooking pot or heavy pan with the stock, thyme, bay leaf, peppercorns, and coriander seeds. Bring just to a boil, then immediately turn down the heat and simmer for 8 minutes.

In the meantime, if using fresh peas, add to a pan of boiling water and blanch for 2 to 3 minutes, depending on size. Drain well. Tip the blanched (or thawed, frozen) peas into a food processor and pulse for a few seconds to crush slightly.

Remove the lamb from the poaching liquid to a warm plate and let rest for 10 minutes.

Tip the crushed peas into a pan and add a generous drizzle of olive oil, the chopped oregano, and salt and pepper to taste. Warm through briefly over medium heat, stirring frequently.

Spoon the peas onto warm serving plates (into a metal ring if you want to shape a neat circle). Slice the lamb into thick pieces and arrange on top. Scatter over a few oregano leaves and add a drizzle of extra virgin olive oil. Sprinkle with sea salt and coarsely ground black pepper to serve.

CRUNCHY GOOSEBERRY CRUMBLE

" Tart green gooseberries are ideal for a crumble, especially if you apply a sweet, crunchy oat topping. Gooseberries vary in acidity, so taste one before cooking to see whether you might need to adjust the amount of sugar in the recipe. **"**

Serves 4
1lb (450g) gooseberries
⅓ cup (75ml) superfine sugar, or to taste

TOPPING:
1½ cups (375ml) crunchy oat cereal or granola
1 tbsp (15ml) raw brown sugar
2 tbsp (30ml) slightly salted butter, cut into small dice

TIP Gooseberries have a relatively short season but they do freeze well and frozen gooseberries, thawed at room temperature, are fine for this crumble. Or you can substitute chopped rhubarb, or a mixture of chopped apples and black currants or blackberries.

Heat the oven to 400°F (200°C) and place a baking sheet inside to heat up. Wash the gooseberries, remove the husks, and pat dry with a clean dish towel.

Tip the gooseberries into a pan, add the sugar, and place over high heat until they begin to release their juices, shaking the pan frequently. Divide the gooseberries among four individual ovenproof dishes.

For the topping, mix the crunchy cereal and raw brown sugar together.

Sprinkle evenly over the gooseberries to cover them and dot with the butter. Bake for about 10 to 15 minutes until the topping is golden brown and the gooseberries are bubbling up around the sides. Let stand for 5 to 10 minutes to cool down slightly before serving.

226

*f*ast

creamy desserts

Banana mousse with butterscotch ripple
White chocolate & cherry mousse
Chocolate fondant
Summer fruit trifles
Baked ricotta with caramelized peaches

Banana mousse with butterscotch ripple

Serves 4

½ cup (125ml) light brown sugar
3 tbsp (45ml) unsalted butter
2¼ cups (550ml) whipping cream, chilled
4 large ripe bananas, ideally chilled in the freezer for 1–2 hours
squeeze of lemon juice
semisweet chocolate, for grating

Put the sugar, butter, and ⅔ cup (150ml) of the cream in a pan over medium heat and stir continuously until the sugar is dissolved and the butter melted. Let bubble for a minute or two, stirring frequently, then remove from the heat and let the sauce cool completely.

Pour the remaining cream into a blender. Peel and chop the bananas and add to the blender along with a squeeze of lemon juice. Whiz until smooth, thick, and creamy.

Spoon a little sauce around the sides of four glasses, smudging some of it for an attractive effect. Divide the banana mousse among the glasses and top with more butterscotch. Use a small teaspoon to ripple the butterscotch through the mousse. Grate over a little semisweet chocolate and chill until ready to serve.

White chocolate & cherry mousse

Serves 4

¼ cup (50ml) superfine sugar
¼ cup (50ml) kirsch or brandy
½ cinnamon stick
4oz (125g) ripe cherries, pitted
7oz (200g) white chocolate
1½ cups (375ml) whipping cream
semisweet chocolate, for grating

Put the sugar, kirsch, ¼ cup (50ml) water, and the cinnamon in a small pan over low heat until the sugar is dissolved, then bring to a boil. Add the cherries and simmer for 3 to 4 minutes until they are tender but still holding their shape. Let cool in the syrup.

Chop the white chocolate into small pieces and tip into a large bowl. Heat a third of the cream in a pan until just beginning to boil, then slowly pour onto the white chocolate, stirring continuously. Keep stirring until all the chocolate has melted. Set aside to cool.

Whip the remaining cream until thick, then fold in the cooled chocolate mixture. Keep whisking to stiff peaks if the combined mixture is not thick enough.

Drain the cherries and set aside 4 for decoration. Divide the rest among individual glasses and pipe or spoon the white chocolate mousse over them. Top each serving with a cherry and grate over some semisweet chocolate to serve.

Chocolate fondant

Serves 4

4 tbsp (60ml) unsalted butter, plus extra
  to grease
2 tsp (10ml) unsweetened cocoa powder,
  to dust
2oz (50g) good quality dark, bittersweet
  chocolate (minimum 70% cocoa solids),
  in pieces
1 large egg
1 large egg yolk
⅓ cup (75ml) superfine sugar
2 tbsp (30ml) Tia Maria liqueur
⅓ cup (75ml) all-purpose flour, sifted
crème fraîche or vanilla ice cream,
  to serve

Heat the oven to 325°F (160°C). Butter 4 ramekins (3 inches/7.5cm in diameter) and dust liberally with cocoa powder. Melt the chocolate and butter in a small bowl set over a pan of hot water, then take off the heat and stir until smooth.

Using an electric whisk, beat the whole egg, egg yolk, and sugar together until pale and thick, then incorporate the chocolate mixture. Fold in the liqueur, followed by the flour.

Divide the chocolate mixture among the ramekins and bake for 12 minutes. Turn the chocolate fondants out onto warm plates and serve immediately with a dollop of crème fraîche or a scoop of vanilla ice cream.

Summer fruit trifles

Serves 4

7oz (200g) strawberries, hulled and
quartered
1⅓lb (600g) other mixed berries (eg
blueberries, blackberries, raspberries)
3 tbsp (45ml) superfine sugar
4oz (125g) amaretti cookies
2½ cups (625ml) good quality ready-
made vanilla custard, chilled

Put the berries and sugar in a nonstick pan and heat
gently for a few minutes until the fruit begins to soften. Transfer to a
bowl and let cool completely. Using a slotted spoon, remove a spoonful
of fruit for the topping and set aside.

Place the amaretti cookies in a deep bowl and lightly
crush with the end of a rolling pin. Reserving a handful, tip the rest into
a large glass bowl (or divide among individual glasses).

Spoon half the custard over the amaretti,
followed by half of the fruit compote. Repeat these layers and top with
a sprinkling of crushed amaretti and the reserved fruit to serve.

Baked ricotta with caramelized peaches

Serves 4

2 tbsp (30ml) butter, plus extra (softened), to grease

⅓ cup (75ml) confectioners' sugar, plus 2 tbsp (30ml) to dust

1lb 2oz (500g) ricotta cheese, drained

2 large eggs

finely grated zest and juice of 1 lemon

3–4 tbsp (45–60ml) superfine sugar, to dredge

4 ripe peaches, pitted and cut into wedges

Heat the oven to 400°F (200°C). Generously butter the base and sides of 4 ramekins, then dust with confectioners' sugar, tilting the ramekins from side to side to ensure an even coating.

Mix the ricotta, eggs, lemon zest, and confectioners' sugar in a large bowl with a fork until evenly combined. Spoon into the ramekins and stand on a baking sheet. Bake for 15 to 20 minutes until golden brown around the edges and quite firm in the middle. Let cool.

Dredge the peach wedges in superfine sugar. Pan-fry in a nonstick skillet with the remaining butter until caramelized. Add the lemon juice, shaking the pan to deglaze. Take off the heat.

Turn out the ricottas onto individual plates. Arrange the caramelized peaches around and spoon over any pan juices to serve.

My favorite time-saving tools

Having the right basic tools in the kitchen can make a big impact on speed and efficiency. A set of sharp knives is essential. Here are a few other time-saving items I can't do without:

Hand-held blender A good professional model with a few variable operating speeds is vital for making velvety smooth soups, vegetable and fruit purées, and smoothies. I also use it to lighten sauces—blitzing directly in the pan means less washing up.

Cook's blowtorch This is brilliant for caramelizing dessert toppings (crème brulée, for example) and it is quicker, more effective, and easier to control than using the broiler. Domestic versions are now relatively inexpensive and easy to find, so if you haven't got one already, treat yourself!

Mandolin No matter how good your knife skills, a mandolin is a handy tool to slice vegetables and fruits quickly and evenly. Although you can get them in wood or stainless steel, my favorite mandolin is a plastic Japanese version with a very sharp blade and a safety hand guard.

Microplane grater This costs more than a standard box grater but its razor-sharp blades will last for many years, saving you time and money in the long run. I use mine to zest citrus fruit and grate all kinds of ingredients, from garlic and ginger to hard cheeses and chocolate.

Food processor or mini-chopper I generally use my food processor to make dough and crumble toppings but it is also useful for fast-chopping vegetables, making curry pastes, even mincing meat.

fast drinks party

{entertaining menu}

We love having friends over for drinks and often find ourselves in the kitchen beforehand, hastily assembling finger foods to serve with Champagne, cocktails, or wine. All of the nibbles on this menu are unbelievably easy and foolproof, but together they are infinitely more impressive than bowls of salty nuts and chips. Serves 10.

Crispy prosciutto with asparagus
Cherry tomato & feta kebabs
Olives wrapped in anchovies
Smoked salmon & horseradish cream on pumperknickel
Minty mojito
Blueberry & pomegranate fizz

- Soften the blueberries and prise out the seeds from the pomegranate.
- Blanch and refresh the asparagus, then roll in the prosciutto.
- Make the tomato and feta kebabs. Wrap the olives in anchovies.
- Assemble the salmon and horseradish cream on pumperknickel.
- Make the minty mojito cocktail.
- Pan-fry the wrapped asparagus spears and keep warm.
- Make the fizz and serve the drinks with the nibbles.

CRISPY PROSCIUTTO WITH ASPARAGUS

" These asparagus rolls are sophisticated enough for a drinks party, but they are just as popular with children. Tana even puts them in the kid's lunchboxes. "

Serves 10

30 asparagus spears, trimmed
sea salt and black pepper
15 slices prosciutto
3–4 tbsp (45–60ml) olive oil

Blanch the asparagus in boiling salted
water for 2 to 3 minutes until bright green and just tender. Drain and refresh under cold running water, then drain again and pat dry.

Cut each prosciutto slice
in half lengthwise and wrap around an asparagus spear.

Pan-fry the asparagus rolls in a
hot pan with a little olive oil, turning frequently, for 2 to 3 minutes until the ham is crisp. Grind over a little pepper and serve.

CHERRY TOMATO & FETA KEBABS

" These are so easy you could get young children to make them. Try drizzling a little balsamic vinegar over the kebabs as you serve them. "

Cut the feta into ¾-inch (2cm) cubes and halve the
cherry tomatoes. Thread them onto toothpicks, sandwiching a feta cube between two tomato halves. Thread a basil leaf onto each end and arrange the kebabs on a serving plate.

Just before serving, drizzle a little extra virgin
olive oil over the kebabs and sprinkle with a little freshly ground pepper.

Serves 10

10oz (300g) feta cheese
30 cherry tomatoes
30 small basil leaves
extra virgin olive oil, to drizzle
black pepper

OLIVES WRAPPED IN ANCHOVIES

❝ Fresh marinated anchovies from the supermarket chiller cabinet are perfect for this nibble. Otherwise use good quality canned anchovy fillets in olive oil. ❞

Serves 10
30 marinated anchovies or anchovy
fillets in olive oil
30 Kalamata olives

Wrap an anchovy fillet around each

olive and secure with a toothpick. Arrange on a platter.

SMOKED SALMON
& HORSERADISH CREAM ON PUMPERNICKEL

❝ Dark pumperknickel bread, with its nutty flavor, sets off savory smoked salmon and creamy horseradish to delicious effect. ❞

Serves 10
½ cup (125ml) crème fraîche
2–3 tbsp (30–45ml) creamed horseradish
sauce
sea salt and black pepper
10 thin slices pumpernickel, toasted
14oz (400g) smoked salmon slices

Mix the crème fraîche and

horseradish sauce together and season with salt and pepper to taste, then spread on top of each slice of toasted pumpernickel. Lay the smoked salmon slices on top and trim the edges to neaten. Cut into bite-size pieces and arrange on a serving platter.

MINTY MOJITO

" This is one of my favorite drinks on vacation by the beach, and it's also fun to make at home. I tend to make my cocktails fairly strong, but you could always add more soda water... or less if you prefer. "

Serves 10
plenty of crushed ice
¾ cup (175ml) superfine sugar
6–8 limes, halved
1 large bunch of mint
generous 1 cup (250ml) white or light rum
about 2 cups (500ml) soda water

Half fill a large pitcher with crushed ice and sprinkle in the sugar. Grate the zest from one of the limes into the pitcher, then squeeze the juice from all of the limes and add to the pitcher. Drop in the spent lime halves that haven't been zested.

Snip the leaves from the bunch of mint into the pitcher and gently crush against the ice with a spoon.

Pour in the rum and add soda water to taste. Stir well and pour into chilled glasses to serve.

BLUEBERRY & POMEGRANATE FIZZ

" I love this fruity Champagne cocktail (illustrated on page 239). For a milder tipple, dilute the fizz with some blueberry and pomegranate juice. Spoon the blueberries and pomegranate seeds into each glass, one-third fill with the fruit juice, and top off with Champagne. "

Heat a skillet until hot, then tip in the blueberries and sugar and add a little splash of water. Place over medium heat for a minute to slightly soften the berries. Tip onto a plate and let cool. Meanwhile, carefully prise out the seeds from the pomegranate, avoiding the bitter membrane.

Put a spoonful of blueberries and a sprinkling of pomegranate seeds into 10 champagne flutes. Pour over the chilled Champagne and serve at once.

Serves 10
5oz (150g) blueberries
2 tsp (10ml) superfine sugar
1 pomegranate
1 bottle of Champagne, well chilled

BASICS

I appreciate the need to take shortcuts, but some convenience foods are strictly off limits—including awful-tasting stock cubes and almost all ready-made sauces in jars. A few basics are really worth the time and effort you spend making them.

A good example is mayonnaise. No commercial variety can ever compare to homemade mayonnaise, both in terms of flavor and consistency. Invariably, commercial mayonnaise is packed with sugar, preservatives, and flavor enhancers—so you are also getting hit with lots of additives.

I'm often asked how the quality of good restaurant food can be replicated at home. I always say: start with the basics. Use good quality stocks and sauces and you are halfway to perfecting a dish. Whenever you have an hour or two to spare, make up a quantity of stock and freeze in smaller amounts, so you always have some on hand. If you run out and need to resort to ready-made alternatives, buy good quality fresh stock in cartons or jars. The other basic recipes here are quick and easy to make—keep in screw-topped jars in the refrigerator to use during the week.

Chicken stock • Fish stock • Vegetable stock
Classic vinaigrette • Mayonnaise • Pesto • Sweet chili dipping sauce

Chicken stock

Makes about 6⅓ cups (1.5 liters)

2 tbsp (30ml) olive oil

1 carrot, peeled and chopped

1 onion, peeled and chopped

2 celery stalks, chopped

1 leek, washed and sliced

1 bay leaf

1 thyme sprig

3 garlic cloves, peeled

2 tbsp (30ml) tomato paste

2 tbsp (30ml) all-purpose flour

2¼lb (1kg) raw chicken bones

sea salt and black pepper

Heat the olive oil in a large stockpot and add the vegetables, herbs, and garlic. Cook over medium heat, stirring occasionally, until the vegetables are golden. Stir in the tomato paste and flour and cook for another minute. Add the chicken bones, then pour in enough cold water to cover. Season lightly. Bring to a boil and skim off any scum that rises to the surface. Reduce the heat and let simmer gently for 1 hour.

Let the stock stand for a few minutes (to cool slightly and allow the ingredients to settle) before passing through a fine strainer. Let cool. Refrigerate and use within 5 days, or freeze the stock in convenient portions for up to 3 months.

Brown chicken stock
Make as above, first roasting the chicken bones at 400°F (200°C) for 20 minutes. This stock lends a greater depth of flavor to a dish.

Fish stock

Makes about 4 cups (1 liter)

2 tbsp (30ml) olive oil

1 small onion, peeled and chopped

½ celery stalk, sliced

1 small fennel bulb, chopped

sea salt and black pepper

2¼lb (1kg) white fish bones and trimmings (or crab or lobster shells)

⅓ cup (75ml) dry white wine

Heat the olive oil in a stockpot and add the onion, celery, fennel, and a little salt and pepper. Stir over medium heat for 3 to 4 minutes until the vegetables begin to soften but not brown. Add the fish bones and trimmings and pour in enough cold water to cover the ingredients. Simmer for 20 minutes, then remove the pan from the heat and let cool.

Ladle the stock through a fine strainer and discard the solids. Refrigerate and use within 2 days, or freeze in smaller quantities for up to 3 months.

Vegetable stock

Makes about 6⅓ cups (1.5 liters)

3 onions, peeled and roughly
   chopped
1 leek, washed and roughly chopped
2 celery stalks, roughly chopped
6 carrots, peeled and roughly
   chopped
1 head of garlic, halved crosswise
1 tsp (5ml) white peppercorns
1 bay leaf
few thyme, basil, tarragon, cilantro,
   and parsley sprigs, tied together
¾ cup (175ml) dry white wine
sea salt and black pepper

Put the vegetables, garlic, peppercorns, and bay leaf in a large stockpot and pour on cold water to cover, about 8½ cups (2 liters). Bring to a boil, lower the heat to a simmer, and let cook gently for 20 minutes. Remove the pan from the heat and add the bundle of herbs, white wine, and a little seasoning. Give the stock a stir and let cool completely.

If you have time, chill the stock overnight before straining. Pass the liquid through a fine strainer. Refrigerate and use within 5 days, or freeze in smaller amounts for up to 3 months.

Classic vinaigrette

Makes about 1 cup (250ml)

⅓ cup (75ml) extra virgin olive oil
⅓ cup (75ml) peanut oil
3 tbsp (45ml) white wine vinegar
½ tsp (2ml) Dijon mustard
sea salt and black pepper

Put the ingredients in a measuring cup and whisk together to emulsify (or use a stick blender to combine).

Pour into a clean squeezy bottle or screw-topped jar and seal. Keep in the refrigerator or cool larder for up to a week. Shake well before each use.

Mayonnaise

Makes about 1¼ cups (300ml)

2 large egg yolks
1 tsp (5ml) white wine vinegar
1 tsp (5ml) English or Dijon
   mustard
sea salt and white pepper
1¼ cups (300ml) peanut oil

Put the egg yolks, vinegar, mustard, and a pinch of salt in a food processor (fitted with a small bowl attachment, if you have one). Whiz for a few minutes until thick and creamy. With the motor running, slowly trickle in the peanut oil in a thin stream until the mayonnaise is thick and emulsified. Season generously with salt and pepper.

Transfer the mayonnaise to a bowl or jar, cover, and refrigerate. Use within 3 days.

note If the mayonnaise splits as you are adding the oil, transfer the mixture to a pitcher. Put another egg yolk, a little mustard, and seasoning into the food processor, and whiz for a minute or two, then slowly add the split mayonnaise. It should re-emulsify.

Pesto

Makes about 1 cup (250ml)

⅓ cup (75ml) pine nuts

large bunch of basil, leaves picked

3 garlic cloves, peeled

2oz (50g) Parmesan, freshly grated

½ cup (125ml) olive oil, plus extra to seal

sea salt and black pepper

Lightly toast the pine nuts in a dry skillet over medium heat, then tip onto a plate and let cool. Put the pine nuts, basil leaves, garlic, and grated Parmesan in a blender or food processor and blitz to a rough paste. With the motor running, slowly pour in the olive oil through the funnel. You will need to stop the machine and scrape down the sides with a spatula a few times. When fully combined, season to taste with salt and pepper.

Transfer the pesto to a screw-topped jar, pour a thin layer of olive oil over the surface, and cover with the lid. It will keep well in the refrigerator for up to a week, particularly if you re-cover the surface with a fresh layer of olive oil after each use.

Sweet chili dipping sauce

Makes ¾–1 cup (175–250ml)

½ cup (125ml) superfine sugar

5 garlic cloves, peeled

2-inch (5cm) piece fresh ginger, peeled and roughly chopped

5–6 long red chiles, seeded and roughly chopped

small handful of cilantro leaves

juice of 2 large limes

2 tbsp (30ml) light soy sauce

2 tbsp (30ml) Thai fish sauce

Put the sugar in a small, heavy pan with about ⅓ cup (75ml) water. Stir over low heat to dissolve the sugar, then bring to a boil. Let bubble for 5 to 8 minutes to reduce and thicken. In the meantime, put the garlic, ginger, red chiles, cilantro, and lime juice in a food processor and pulse for a few seconds to a coarse paste.

When the sugar syrup has reached a light golden color, carefully add the spice paste, standing back as the caramel will splutter and spit. Stir in the soy and fish sauces. Return to a boil, then immediately take the pan off the heat and let cool completely. Pour into a clean jar, refrigerate, and use within a week.

INDEX

ACKNOWLEDGMENTS

I owe my thanks to the talented, dedicated team who, once again, have worked so hard to produce this quality book: Mark Sargeant, Emily Quah, Jill Mead, Helen Lewis, and Janet Illsley. I am especially grateful to Pat Llewellyn and everyone at Optomen TV for producing another great series, and to Anne Furniss and Alison Cathie of Quadrille, for publishing the book to accompany it. Also to Jo Barnes for her determination to make this book another huge success.

As ever, I'm truly appreciative of everyone at Gordon Ramsay Holdings, from Gillian Thomson to Chris Hutcheson. And last but not least, a big thank you to my wife, Tana, and our wonderful children: Megan, Jack, Holly, and Tilly.

Editorial director **Anne Furniss**
Art director **Helen Lewis**
Project editor **Janet Illsley**
Photographer **Jill Mead**
Food stylist **Mark Sargeant**
Home economist **Emily Quah**
Assistant designer **Katherine Case**
Editorial assistant **Andrew Bayliss**
Production **Vincent Smith, Ruth Deary**

Optomen Television:
Managing director **Patricia Llewellyn**
Executive producer, F Word **Ben Adler**
Executive producer **Jon Swain**
Series editor **Deborah Sargeant**
Assistant producer **Lauren Abery**

Optomen Television Limited
1, Valentine Place
London SE1 8QH
www.optomen.com

First published in 2007 by Quadrille Publishing Ltd
Alhambra House, 27-31 Charing Cross Road,
London WC2H 0LS
www.quadrille.co.uk
Text © 2007 Gordon Ramsay
Photography © 2007 Jill Mead
Design and layout © 2007 Quadrille Publishing Ltd
Format and program © 2007 Optomen Television Ltd

Library and Archives Canada Cataloguing in Publication Data

Ramsay, Gordon
    Gordon Ramsay's fast food : recipes from the
f word / Gordon Ramsay.

ISBN 978-1-55470-064-6

    1. Quick and easy cookery. I. Title.
TX833.5.R35 2008   641.5'55   C2007-905373-4

THE CANADA COUNCIL | LE CONSEIL DES ARTS
FOR THE ARTS | DU CANADA
SINCE 1957 | DEPUIS 1957

ONTARIO ARTS COUNCIL
CONSEIL DES ARTS DE L'ONTARIO

The publisher gratefully acknowledges the support of the Canada Council for the Arts and the Ontario Arts Council for its publishing program. We acknowledge the support of the Government of Ontario through the Ontario Media Development Corporation's Ontario Book Initiative.

We acknowledge the financial support of the Government of Canada through the Book Publishing Industry Development Program (BPIDP) for our publishing activities.

Key Porter Books Limited
Six Adelaide Street East, Tenth Floor
Toronto, Ontario
Canada M5C 1H6

www.keyporter.com

Printed and bound in China
08 09 10 11 12 6 5 4

The author would like to thank The Shop at Bluebird, London SW3 and Ted Baker for supplying clothes for photography.